I Do.

I *Do:*

A Wedding Planner Tells Tales

Lynda Barness

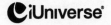

I DO:
A WEDDING PLANNER TELLS TALES

iUniverse books may be ordered through booksellers or by contacting:

iUniverse
1663 Liberty Drive
Bloomington, IN 47403
www.iuniverse.com
1-800-Authors (1-800-288-4677)

ISBN: 978-1-4917-6179-3 (sc)
ISBN: 978-1-4917-6180-9 (e)

Library of Congress Control Number: 2015904622

Print information available on the last page.

iUniverse rev. date: 4/28/2015

Contents

Introduction

It was a classic case of serendipity. In fact, I never expected to be a wedding planner. Never even thought about it.

Sometimes I think it is Barbie's fault.

Barbie the doll, that is. What I remember the most about the Barbie doll from my childhood is that my mother made several outfits for her, and the one I remember and loved the best was a wedding gown. It never occurred to me back then, and indeed, it took me decades to even pose the question, why would my mother have made a bridal gown for a child's doll? The magic of weddings—or at least the magic of being a bride—was introduced early, and I guess it never left me.

Of course, there have been a lot of years between that dress and today. I married right after college, had two terrific daughters, and was divorced a decade later. I ended up in my family's real estate development business, and I loved both the people I worked with and the business itself. But around 2004, I began to see changes in our market, so I made the tough decision to sell the business that had been in my family for eighty years. I sold it in the summer of 2005, right before the bubble burst.

I knew that I would eventually find and become active in another profession, but it was so emotional—and so complicated—to get out of the one I was in that at first I dealt only with the task in front of me. Meanwhile, my daughters grew up and became women, and while I was still extricating myself from real estate, the older one became engaged. Her dad and I hired a full-service wedding planner, but I still enjoyed being involved in a lot of the details. The wedding weekend was a joy from start to finish, but naturally, it was not without emotion—my first *baby* was getting *married!* (And for the record, I felt exactly the same way when my second baby was getting married.)

About a month later came the moment that changed everything. I picked up the Temple University course catalog and just happened upon a noncredit course offering called Wedding Planning and Consulting Certificate Program. I'd had so much fun planning my daughter's wedding that I registered as a lark. I figured that since I had another daughter and two nieces, I would take the course and learn everything that I didn't know the first time around.

The course included numerous guest speakers, so we got to hear firsthand from cake bakers, photographers, invitation specialists, lighting experts, and other seasoned professionals in the field. There were also many wedding planners who came to speak to the class, and some of them offered internships, so I jumped at the opportunity. One wedding consultant, Mark Kingsdorf, became my generous mentor. He allowed me to choose which weddings I wanted to help with, and I tried to vary the locations, the religions (or lack thereof), and the team of wedding professionals as much as possible.

I was looking for wide exposure to the entire wedding industry, and I got it. I worked on seven weddings as an intern and learned about all sorts of issues involved with logistics, timing, and working with clients, as well as some small but important tricks of the trade. For example, before the ceremony, Mark always instructed his interns to place programs on the seats for the bridal party and packets of tissues on the seats for the mothers, and he always had us stand with the bridal party and parents and offer them Listerine mint strips right before they went down the aisle. This was one of my all-time favorite tips, and I still do this at every wedding. You'd be surprised by how thrilled people always are to have a mint at this particular moment.

I also learned how to keep an eye on the big picture and the small details at the same time. For example, even if the setup for the reception initially looks perfect, I always count the seats at each table to make sure that the number matches the seating chart that I've been given, and I check each place setting to make sure that everyone has the appropriate flatware for every course. I am always amazed by how often there is a discrepancy! And I learned that if you have a rainy wedding day, a tent or indoor venue alone will not solve your problems; you need umbrellas—lots of them—not just for keeping the couple dry but also to help ferry guests and assist the wedding party in getting photos. (These days, I have umbrellas that say I DO on them ready and waiting for just such occasions.) I also learned many valuable lessons, including Wedding Planning Lesson #1: wear comfortable shoes! If you are on your feet for twelve hours a day at a wedding, as all wedding planners are, even ballet flats won't cut it—you need both flat heels *and* support. After my first wedding as an intern, I was ready to crawl home. These days, I wear lovely black satin sneakers, and I advise all my assistants and interns to do the same.

During this time, I was also asked to do three weddings all on my own, just by word of mouth. The first couple to approach me was close friends with my married daughter. The second couple was friends with the first, and the groom happened to be very well known in Philadelphia circles. They were married in a high-profile venue with a lot of local media coverage, and they generously put my name in the newspaper as their planner. (This was a tented wedding, and at the time, I knew nothing about wedding tents—so I went back to Temple University to take an actual class called Wedding Tents. Yes, fortunately, that class does exist.) The third wedding was for the daughter of a fellow member of a board of trustees on which I served. I was having a ball, and by the end of that year, I knew that I had found my next calling. I had honed my skills and had a vision for how I wanted to do things, so I felt ready to open the doors of I DO Wedding Consulting. The rest, as they say, is history.

I started collecting wedding stories while doing my very first wedding as an intern, and I did it mainly as a learning tool for myself so that I would remember what had worked and what didn't, what emergency-kit items I'd used, and which wedding professionals and special touches really made for a memorable day. I also did it to remind myself of the funny, poignant, emotional, and challenging parts of my new career. Whenever I needed a pep talk or a laugh or even just a reminder of why I love this job, I could revisit these memories and ·

see just how far I had come and remember all the great moments along the way.

The truth is that I love being a wedding planner. I find the business both challenging and exciting, and I love all the new people I get to meet, as well as the different places and things that I get to see and do. I love putting together what I call the "pieces of a wedding-day puzzle" and working with couples who are eager to teach me about their personal customs, beliefs, and histories and to share their visions, desires, hopes, and dreams. I am personally enriched by every wedding I plan, and I am grateful for the generosity of the families with whom I am privileged to work on such a thrilling and important day. I also enjoy the camaraderie of other wedding professionals and the satisfaction of returning to venues in which I've worked time and time again, knowing that I can count on my amazing colleagues there to make the day a huge success. But a wedding at a new venue can be even more invigorating because it offers me a fresh opportunity to expand my expertise and hone my craft. After all these years, I still find every single wedding incredibly stimulating and, yes, fun (at least most of the time).

My experience over the past ten years has brought me more stories than I can share in these pages. I have now planned close to two hundred weddings, and without these notes, I could never have recalled all the issues, joys, frustrations, and mishaps that I have seen firsthand and that this book exposes. The anecdotes presented here are real stories from real people—brides, grooms, and family members just like you who dreamed of having a perfect, singularly beautiful wedding. The takeaway, though, is that as unique as your wedding was, is, or will be, it is also just like any other in that everything may *not* go perfectly and according to plan. Every wedding, no matter how expensive or flawlessly orchestrated, comes with its share of surprises.

A priest once told me, "In spite of all the planning, something mysterious happens at a wedding." As a planner, I have seen that "mystery" unfold again and again—the amazing outpouring of love from friends and family and the electric current of energy and optimism that surrounds the happy couple and all the people they love best. These feelings transcend the color of the tablecloths or the kinds of flowers in the bouquet or the grumpy bridesmaid in the corner. I always remind my clients who are caught up in the throes of wedding stress that a wedding is only five hours in a lifetime, and those five hours will be wonderful, magical, and memorable no matter what. Your wedding will be yours, and it will be forever special, because it marks the start of your life as one half of a married couple. It will be perfect, even with its imperfections. So take a deep breath, relax, and enjoy the ride.

Two days before her only daughter's wedding, I received this e-mail from a client:

> *Just a few moments ago a rainbow stayed in my driving path for quite a while. I understand the physics of rain and light but can also appreciate the meaning of serendipity and "symbols." Such omens are not to be ignored. To the best team a family could have in launching a new family, thank you for helping us experience rainbows and other magical moments.*

And to all my clients, an enormous thank-you, as well. Your enthusiasm, creativity, and trust are what make this job such a pleasure. I know how fortunate I am to be able to do something I love and to help others at such a special, joyous time in their lives. Lucky me. I am so grateful.

I hope that you enjoy these vignettes.

Lynda Barness

1. A Day in the Life of a Wedding Planner

Behind the Scenes at I DO Wedding Consulting

*T*he biggest compliment that I can get after a wedding is to have a mother question why she even bothered to hire a planner since everything went so smoothly. Of course, it's *because* she hired a planner that the day went well! It's my job to make even the most spectacular wedding look effortless and to make sure that the entire event runs like clockwork. But the truth is that there are many, many hours of thought, legwork, logistical planning, attention to detail, and oversight that my team and I put into every single wedding we do. In fact, most weddings start out like the one described in the following e-mail that I received from a bride-to-be:

> *The main thing that I am stressed about is actually … everything! I really want our wedding to be beautiful and unforgettable. I want things to go smoothly and for the whole motif to flow together. I also want to have some little unique details that will make the whole celebration pop. I have no idea about*

> *flowers or the cake, I have looked at many pictures and found things that I like, but I'm afraid that my ideas don't go together. I'm having some modifications done to my dress, and I am TERRIFIED that it will not turn out how I hope and that I will end up hating it. I'm rambling right now, but if you know of any way to calm me down and not have me stress and overthink this whole thing, please let me know!*

From the moment that my clients approach me, it's my job to help them create order out of chaos. I take all their ideas, dreams, and concerns and combine them in a way that works with their logistical needs (how many people are coming, where do they want to have the wedding) as well as practical realities (budget, or the fact that having a wedding in an old historic church with no air-conditioning in the middle of August might not be the best idea). I am a buffer between family factions with differing visions or needs—mothers and fathers, parents and in-laws, siblings, and sometimes even the bride and groom. I play the roles of wedding expert, problem solver, counselor, coach, and always reassuring comforter equally throughout the planning process. As one bride said to me, "Lynda, you are my Prozac!"

But before I even take on a client (and I have always had multiple clients at the same time), there is a lot of work to do on the business front. I strive to keep my mind open, my ideas fresh and creative, and to stay up to date on the wedding industry. I am constantly talking to people about weddings they've attended, and I hear the stories of things they loved and the things they thought were ridiculous. I purchase all the wedding magazines each month and then sit down and read them all in one long sitting so that I have a sense of the developing trends, and I look for inspiration everywhere—on the Internet, in store windows, in nonwedding magazines, on blogs, and even when I travel. I update my own website with photos from the weddings I do, write for wedding blogs, and submit my clients' weddings to magazines. I also do a good deal of networking. Since I recommend specific wedding professionals (photographers, DJs, caterers, and the like) to clients all the time, it is important that I get to know as many as possible. In the months when there are typically fewer weddings—in the Philadelphia area, that often means January, February, and March—I meet with a lot of wedding professionals for coffee, breakfast, or lunch so that we can get to know each other. These personal relationships really matter when it comes to executing a fantastic wedding because you always want a great team working alongside you.

All of this, of course, is in addition to the hands-on work of actually planning a client's wedding. As soon as I am hired, I start a timeline for each wedding, and this becomes the master document into which all the ideas, information, choices, decisions, small details, and vendor information for each particular event get entered. I collect all the contracts for the venue, photographer, florist, musicians, and so on; obviously, I am not an attorney, so I don't read them for legal content, but I do take timing and other information from them that helps me to make a larger plan for the big day. I revise and revise the timeline with input from wedding professionals and clients throughout the months and weeks leading up to the event until I have a highly detailed road map for the entire day that outlines *exactly* how the wedding is to unfold. My goal is to have every detail in one document, which can then be shared with the couple, their families, the bridal party, and the wedding professionals with whom we are working. I check and recheck everything ("Check and double-check" is my middle name, along with "What if?") to make sure that everyone is on the same page. Some of the details that I include may seem silly—for example, that the bride is planning to pin a family brooch on her bouquet—but I list it as a reminder to the photographer that she will be carrying something special that he/she may want to capture. My timelines for a wedding weekend are typically about ten pages long (although my all-time record, which was for an at-home tented wedding on a gorgeous estate, was twenty-seven). I always tell people that they can take my timeline and extract what they need and delete everything else—but it's vitally important that everyone has a chance to see the plan for the wedding as a whole.

I also meet with my clients throughout the planning process so that I can get to know the couple and their families, go over details, and answer any questions they may have. These meetings are always interesting and fun, and I truly enjoy this part of the job. Sometimes the clients and I get together with other vendors or wedding professionals, as well, so that I can be privy to the conversation, know what decisions are made, and offer advice if needed.

Then, of course, there is the actual wedding weekend. I attend the rehearsal, and then I have a team of wedding directors who work alongside me on the day of the event itself. No matter how carefully we've planned up until this point, we try to be prepared for every contingency, and I travel to each wedding with an extensive emergency kit. My kit started out with the obvious items that are recommended in any wedding magazine—a sewing kit, scissors, fashion tape, and the like—but over the years, I have been asked for many unusual items that I now make sure to have with me no matter what. Chalk, a thong, earplugs, duct tape, a crochet hook, and Febreze are just some of the unexpected items that I have found can come in handy when you are trying to solve a problem five minutes before the wedding starts.

So much of what a wedding planner does on the day of the wedding is never seen by anyone, and as a result, our work often looks organic and easy. Ha! Here is an example of what I did for *just one* wedding—from the moment I arrived at the venue at ten o'clock in the morning:

◊ made sure there were bar stools in the bridal suite so the women had a comfortable place for hair and makeup (and so that it would be comfortable for the stylists too)
◊ steamed five bridesmaids' dresses and five gray pashminas (I had to go and find the pashminas in a room downstairs)
◊ used sandpaper on the bride's and bridesmaids' shoes to prevent slipping
◊ put champagne on ice in the bridal suite

◊ placed straws near the drinks area for bridesmaids (so they wouldn't disturb their lipstick after hair and makeup)

◊ went to find the flowers for the bride and the mother of the bride

◊ gave the father of the bride, groom, and groomsmen their boutonnieres and pinned them on

◊ spoke to photographer and went over the shot list for the day

◊ cleaned the bride's shoes with white chalk (She had stepped in something and asked for help because the shoes had crystals on the bottoms that spelled out "I Do" and were supposed to be photographed.)

◊ carried two cases of water from the kitchen to the front of the venue for guests who were there early for family photos—pretzels too

◊ was present while family portraits were being done; distributed bobby pins and fashion tape for the groom's father's cummerbund

◊ dealt with the bus driver regarding a complicated schedule

◊ coordinated the delivery and setup of chairs for the ceremony

◊ confirmed cake delivery with catering manager

◊ checked the coatrack and hangers by the ballroom and brought in extra hangers from another coat check

◊ put the card catcher out

◊ opened boxes with the white metal bowls and placed the yarmulkes (head coverings for

Jewish men) in them and put them on a table
where they would be accessible for the guests

◊ placed programs on every other chair for the
ceremony

◊ put reserved seat signs on the front rows of chairs
and gave a reserved table sign to the caterer

◊ moved one row of chairs to the other side of
the room so that the chuppah (the canopy in a
Jewish wedding) would look centered

◊ put the kiddush cup and a glass for the groom to
step on at the end of the ceremony on the table
under the chuppah

◊ got wine for the kiddush cup and poured it

◊ made sure the *ketubah* (the Jewish marriage
license) was moved to the signing site along with
supplies to frame it prior to the ceremony

◊ checked to make sure that the microphone was
on the stand for the rabbi

◊ put amenity baskets in the restrooms

◊ greeted ceremony musicians

◊ called the rabbi when he wasn't there on time—
turns out he was in another part of the building

◊ talked to the bandleader about the mother-son
dance (They had chosen "I Will Always Love
You" by Whitney Houston, but the bandleader
felt it was a breakup song, so I conferred quickly
with the bride and groom after the ketubah
signing, and they decided that mother-son
would join the father-daughter dance of "Love"
by Nat King Cole. Informed the bandleader.)

◊ made sure grandmother and grandfather were
escorted to their seats

◊ lined up the bridal party for the procession

7

◊ cued musicians

◊ made sure the heat lamps were turned on for the cocktail hour

◊ put personalized napkins and swizzle sticks on the bar

◊ put flameless candles on the steps up to the cocktail reception (ninety-eight total!) and turned them on (the florist was supposed to do this but he didn't have enough helpers)

◊ once the cocktail hour had started, checked the ballroom to make sure that seat count for each table was correct and informed the catering manager that several tables didn't have the correct number of chairs and place settings

◊ checked that the floral centerpieces were placed in appropriate places (sometimes there are both high and low arrangements, so we assess to make sure that the room looks interesting and balanced)

◊ checked all candles on the tables to make sure they were not dripping, that all were staying up straight, that they were securely set into the holders, and that there was *no* chance that the flowers would ignite (I only needed one such bad experience to now always check the work of anyone who touches a dining table!)

◊ asked for the lights to be brought down

◊ took pictures of the entire setup to show the mother of the bride

◊ helped guests find their table numbers

◊ dealt with band issues: went over the timeline with the musicians and sound technicians, coordinated the bride and groom's entrance, confirmed the couple's updated first dance choice, passed out parking passes, and reminded the band to announce that the photo booth was open

◊ determined with the catering manager that cake cutting should take place on the table where the cake was already located

◊ cued the bride and groom for their entrance in the reception

◊ during the reception, retrieved the bride's lip gloss and hairspray from her room

I am usually scheduled to leave after the cake cutting, but at this particular wedding, a number of the toasts ran so long that I didn't end up leaving until after eleven o'clock at night. The groom said to me afterward that there were times that he couldn't find me. That was probably because I was *working*!

Being a wedding planner is a lot like being a juggler, because you have to focus on a lot of moving parts at the same time. You need to be able to see the big picture as well as the small details and make sure that everything fits together in a way that works. When a wedding is a smooth and happy experience for the couple, and when everyone is so caught up in the moment that they lose themselves in the celebration and forget that I'm even there, that's when I know that I've done a good job. I also know that I've been successful when I receive e-mails like this one from the mother of a bride whose wedding I had helped plan several years before:

> *Our other daughter's boyfriend just asked for our blessing, and he is going to propose when*

> *they are on vacation next month. You were the*
> *first person I thought of as my mind started*
> *racing in preparation for another wonderful*
> *wedding. I just thought I'd give you a heads*
> *up so that we can get started as soon as*
> *possible after the proposal, since they don't*
> *want to have a long engagement. I would not*
> *do a wedding without you!*

As soon as one wedding ends, another one begins, and that's what makes this business so exciting. Being a wedding planner is *more* than a full-time job, but I love every minute of it, despite the occasional craziness. In its best moments, it's just plain fun. Welcome to my world!

2. *The Family Tree*

Squabbles, Secrets, and Other Complications

I met one mother of the bride for the first time at the wedding rehearsal the night before the wedding. She was very cordial, but she told me that she had only heard that I was involved in her daughter's wedding two weeks earlier—and yet the bride and I had been working together for over a year. I smiled politely, but I couldn't help thinking, *I wonder what the backstory is here?*

Every family has a backstory, and there is something about the pressures of a wedding—both the planning process and the event itself—that brings these stories and emotions to the fore. And as the wedding planner, I'm right in the middle. Like a confessor or therapist (or even a hair stylist), I hear everything. People feel safe talking and sharing or venting to me when they want to get something off their chest. Here are just some of the things that I have heard from clients:

> "Is there any way that my fiancé and I can meet with you alone? My parents are driving us crazy."

Lynda Barness

"We feel very disconnected from everything because my mom has been making plans without consulting us, and we haven't been included in most of the decisions."

"My parents think that this is their wedding and have told us that they get the final say on EVERYTHING, even my dress and the members of our wedding party! How do other brides and grooms handle this type of behavior?"

"I'm not trying to put you in the middle, but I know that my dad values your opinion, and I don't think that my fiancé and I should have to forfeit one little request due to his lack of knowledge and inability to see this as OUR wedding rather than a reflection of him!"

"My parents are driving us NUTS. Seriously, this has been the most painful process ever (and believe it or not, I've sheltered you from most of the emails, fights, etc!)."

"We have a couple of people (I'm sure you can guess who they are) who have strong opinions about how the beginning of the reception should go, and my fiancé and I can no longer muster the strength to care. So here is the new order ..."

"I will look at the seating chart later today and get back to you, although I am happy with whatever everyone else thinks is best, as long as I am not sitting near:
1. The loudspeaker
2. My mother."

But I also get an earful from the mothers themselves:

"Quite frankly, my daughter and I are at each other's throats, so she needs to either step up and return my calls, or stop whining!"

"Things are going okay, but I wanted to tell you that I've given up on the 'Ave Maria' thing. As my friends would say, 'That's not the hill I want to die on.'"

"Can you handle the bride for me? Because I can't take it anymore!"

I personally experienced the maelstrom of family opinions, expectations, and emotions during the planning of my first daughter's wedding. From the differing visions (the couple wanted a small destination wedding on a beach, and we ended up with 347 guests in a large local venue), to what wines to serve and the menu itself (no cilantro!), *all* of us—the bride, groom, parents, stepparents, and siblings—learned to practice the art of negotiation and compromise. And in retrospect, the big question—"Whose wedding is it, anyway?"—was weighted a bit too heavily on the side of the parents. I think about this a lot in hindsight and wish I had been more aware of it then. It is something that everyone—especially the parents of the couple—needs to keep in mind throughout the planning process. I make a special effort to encourage all the parents I work with to prioritize the wishes of the bride and groom when making decisions.

Beyond that, I do whatever I can to keep the peace while still moving the process forward. Instead of playing therapist (which I'm not qualified to do) or trying to solve issues that may have been going on for years, I try to embrace my role as a mediator and get everyone to focus on how we can make the *wedding* a success. When emotions are running high, it's my job to calm everyone down. Often this simply means acknowledging the different viewpoints and guiding the various parties toward a compromise or a solution. It helps that I am usually viewed as a neutral party, and that my "expert" advice is based on my experience from so many weddings. That said, there have been times when the talks have broken down, and I've been called upon to stand in for clients who are at the end of their rope. One bride e-mailed her parents and fiancé to tell them, "Unfortunately, I am feeling extremely stressed out by all of this, so I am going to let Lynda make the call for me and sign off on all future wedding decisions." And once I even received an e-mail that said:

> *After everything we discussed, we have decided to go to Las Vegas and have a small ceremony so that we don't have to deal with any of our family members and their issues!*

One thing I know for certain is that weddings truly have the ability to touch us all and to show us the power of a family's love and relationships. I experienced this with the weddings of both of my daughters, and I witness it again and again at every wedding that I help plan. But, as we know, families are quirky, relationships are complicated, emotions run high, and yes, mistakes are made. Many are made with love, but they are still made. My best advice to all my clients is to take a deep breath, keep your eyes on the prize, and remember that you love these people. On the day of your wedding, focus on the person you are marrying and appreciate that the members of your extended families—however imperfect they may be—have all come together and pitched in to help you celebrate your love for each other and make the day as special as it can be. They may drive you crazy, but their love is a part of what has gotten you to this amazing moment. So hold on to that thought and smile, even as they raise their glasses and toast you with the champagne you didn't want to the music of the band that wasn't your first choice. These details will likely be forgotten, but the great hope at any wedding is that the bond between you, your spouse, and your two families will be with all of you for many years to come.

One bride told me this story. She went shopping for her wedding gown on several occasions with her friends. She found a dress she absolutely loved. When her mother returned from a trip out of town, the bride took her to see the dress of her dreams—and her mother *hated* it. She told the bride it made her look fat (which was ridiculous since the bride was tiny) and ultimately said that if the bride bought the dress, she (the mother) wouldn't attend her daughter's wedding! Believe it or not, the daughter capitulated, and she purchased and wore the dress of her mother's choice.

I've had several brides tell me they were trying to get pregnant before the wedding—but they always said, "Don't tell my mother!"

At the very end of our first meeting, one bride informed me that she and her fiancé had actually eloped to Scotland over the summer and were already married. They knew that their families would want a big wedding, however, so no one else knew—and they weren't planning on telling anyone for, oh, twenty years.

One mother of the groom—who wasn't actually my client—called me up and said, "My husband and I went to someone's party last week, and we realized that we hadn't invited them to the wedding. Could you call them and introduce yourself and ask if they're coming, and then apologize when they say that they never received the invitation?"

The groom's parents were throwing the engagement party, and the groom's mother had hired a photographer. Although I didn't have anything to do with the planning of this party, I reminded her to give a list to the photographer of the people she wanted in the photos. Afterward, she told me that she had been too busy to do this ... and there were *no* photos of the bride's parents! What was she thinking? And Mr. Photographer, what were *you* thinking? Or was there more to this story?

For the wedding, however, the mother of the groom gave the (different) photographer a shot list a mile long, and yet, she was twenty minutes late for the pictures. I still have no idea what she was doing, because her hair and makeup had been done earlier in the day.

Once at a reception, I saw an older woman staggering around, swearing at some man. The man walked away from her, and she toppled over and then slid down to lie on the floor. Fortunately, the man returned and removed her. I spoke with the catering manager, and we discussed the bartender cutting people off (which most bartenders do regularly—apparently several other guests had already been cut off by this time, even though it was early in the evening and the dinner hadn't yet been served). The manager called security to make sure the woman left, but it was an ugly scene.

I worked with a florist who was spectacular, but he was hard to reach the week before the wedding. The father of the bride contacted me several times about this, and I too tried to contact the florist, to no avail. The father said to me, "I have been known as a genius, so I understand genius. But we still need to get the information from the florist." This is the same father who told me he wasn't used to writing small checks and usually wrote them "in the millions, not thousands."

One mother of the groom gave a toast and a blessing at the reception, and she said that the bride was "like a daughter" to her, which was very nice and which many mothers-in-law say. But the actual mother of the bride freaked. She left the reception in hysterics and went to the catering manager's office in the venue's basement. She was saying that she felt she had lost her daughter. Talk about drama! Fortunately, the father was finally able to retrieve his wife and bring her back upstairs.

Shortly afterward, this mother came up to me and asked why the food hadn't been served. While she was out of the room, she missed two courses. I assured her that the salad and soup courses had already been served and that we were exactly on schedule. She then told me that the older folks had left, and she demanded to know why dinner was being served at ten o'clock at night. I gently reminded her that it was only nine o'clock and that we were right in sync with the schedule we had planned together weeks before. The poor woman was on edge about everything, and I did my best to help her relax and enjoy the party.

One groom's brother made a very inappropriate speech/toast at the reception that talked about how the groom used to suck toothpaste out of a bottle like he was sucking "on his mother's boob."

About two weeks before the wedding, the mother of the groom was going crazy with all the things she had left to do. What things? She had the bathroom amenity baskets to create (which basically meant a trip to the drugstore, since she already had the hatboxes) … and she had to fold the cake boxes for the giveaway at the end of the night … and she had to tie the programs with ribbons (she had ordered 400 programs for 351 guests). I suggested that the stationer who was creating the programs tie the ribbons, and I even offered to go to the drugstore to shop and also fold the cake boxes for her—which I was not excited to do—but she was so frantic that she was driving her husband nuts. And the crazy thing is that she wouldn't let me do any of it! She just couldn't give up the control. The father of the groom confided to me during planning process, "I now *really* understand the concept of elopement."

At our initial meeting, it became clear that there was a tug-of-war going on between the bride's parents, who were divorced. The parents had agreed to split the cost of the wedding, but the mother had a fixed number in mind. It was clear to me that the father was trying to show up the mother and make her look cheap. He told me that he wanted to hire the most expensive band in the city, which definitely didn't fit into the mother's budget. The father and bride had an argument about this in front of me, and the bride stormed off.

One father of the bride gave a very long speech. At the house that morning, he asked if would be okay to *read* his speech in front of everyone at the wedding, and I encouraged him to do so. At the wedding, he never even took out his notes, and his speech went on and on. I always give the same advice (paraphrasing Roosevelt): be brief, be sincere, be seated!

One matron of honor gave a speech that made me cringe. She talked about how she and the bride used to talk when they were younger about how they were going to grow up and get married to a doctor or an engineer (the bride got the engineer), how their husbands were going to support a lavish lifestyle, and how they would live next door to each other and eat bonbons all day. It was hard to tell if the matron of honor was attempting to be humorous or complaining when she went on to say that she wasn't moving into a mansion anytime soon.

One father of the bride gave a speech that was so long and rambling that we had to skip a dance set after the appetizer to get back on schedule. Clients take note: if something runs long, the *only* place you can steal time is from the dancing and partying.

In my initial meeting with one family, the bride was discussing the fact that she and the groom did not want a wedding cake. Instead, they wanted a pie station with at least four selections. Someone said to the bride, "Well, what are you going to cut?"

The father of the bride responded, without a hesitation, "My wrists!"

One bride and groom I worked with had been very budget conscious during the planning process. At the tasting, the bride's mother came over to me and talked about all the extras she wanted: chargers, upgraded chairs, and more. She said that she would just write a check for everything she wanted and told me not to tell her husband. Believe it or not, I had heard this before.

I once had a lot of drama toward the end of the cocktail reception, when the groom's brother (who was also the best man) created a scene. The hotel closed the bars for about five or ten minutes at the end of the cocktail hour so that the guests would go right into the ballroom. The bars would then reopen, there would be wine service at the tables, and the servers would also take drink orders from the guests.

Well, someone told the best man that he couldn't have another drink at the bar because it was closing for a short time. He grabbed a bottle of vodka, pulled off the pouring spout, and started chugging directly from the bottle. Foul language ensued, and so did a visit from management.

I should have known that there was trouble ahead when I met the *groom's* parents—who were my clients—for the very first time, and they talked badly about the bride's family. It was clear that they saw themselves as sophisticated and in the know. They actually told me that their future in-laws were like the Beverly Hillbillies. On top of that, they hired me but didn't tell the *bride* for quite a while that a wedding consultant was going to be involved. But when I finally met the bride's family, they were absolutely lovely. There were issues along the way, and the bride and her family were always the ones who bent over backward to keep the peace.

One mother of the groom insisted that she wanted to pick the florist and sniffed that she didn't want "any dandelions on the table."

The father of the groom, who was Jewish, wanted a "minimum of ethnic overtones." He said, "I don't want this to be a Jewish folk fest." He and his wife also asked what I thought about doing two separate invitations, one for their side and one for the bride's, because the bride wanted both Hebrew and English on the invitation, and the groom's family was against this. They also wanted *black tie* on their invitations, while the bride's family did not. I gently suggested that they do one invitation since they were bringing two families together, not separating them. The result? The groom's mother had two sets of invitations made.

The mother of the groom, who was planning the wedding, put a monogram on the wedding programs ... except she knew that the bride was keeping her maiden name. She proceeded to do the same with the place cards and the bathroom paper towels.

The name issue emerged again when we all had a meeting a few weeks before the wedding. I was there with the parents of the groom, the bride, and her mother, and I asked the bride how she and the groom wanted to be introduced at the beginning of the reception. The bride responded that she just wanted to use their first names. The mother of the groom made a huge deal about it and made it clear that she wanted them introduced as Mr. and Mrs. Ultimately, the bride gave in. She was good-natured and felt it was in everyone's interest to keep the peace.

Once I was asked to guard the hallway to make sure that no children came into the reception. The mother of the bride was one of fourteen children, so lots and lots of family were at the hotel. There were, however, no incidents.

I once met with a mom and her daughter who proceeded to debate every issue right in front of me. The mom wanted a major blowout, while the bride wanted a smaller, intimate wedding. The conversation was very spirited, to say the least, with the daughter threatening to elope.

Here is an e-mail regarding a seating chart that circulated among family members and on which I was copied:

> *The seating chart has flaws. Unless you want your ceremony to have pyrotechnics and fireworks to rival any July 4th celebration, I wouldn't recommend putting the two brothers together. They may be able to behave for the*

> *45 minutes—then again, maybe not—but by the end, they will both be racing to the bar and be obnoxious for the next few hours. I would put their sister in between them, although the* bride's *sister in between them would be even better in terms of keeping things calm and happy. But it's up to you.*

At eleven thirty on the morning of the wedding, I found the groom's mother slouched on the floor. I didn't know if she was hungover from the rehearsal dinner, just exhausted, sick, or what, but I did the only thing I could think of and volunteered to take her to a private space to nap.

At one introductory meeting with a bride and groom, it was immediately clear that there were some major issues. The bride didn't let the groom get a word in edgewise, and when he went to get a drink at the Starbucks counter, she told me that he could never follow through on plans, had good ideas but no execution, and complained that he could have surprised her one hundred times with an engagement ring but instead he just handed it to her after dinner. She also made a lot of snide comments about his mother. In hindsight, it would have been better for me if I hadn't taken on this family as clients.

Fast-forward to the day of the wedding. The bride and groom were snipping at each other all day long.

She put him down verbally in front of the photographer and videographer, berated him for not reminding her to bring her bouquet for the introductions at the reception, shoved him during the hora, and at cake-cutting time, she grabbed the knife out of his hands. In my ten years of doing weddings, I have never seen such behavior either during the process of wedding planning or on the wedding day.

At the hotel before the wedding, the bride's father told me that he wanted to add another person to the toast list and that he wanted another of his friends to do a Jewish blessing over the bread (even though the bride's family was *not* Jewish). I had to find the banquet manager to locate a loaf of bread, and I had to alert the band of the new toast order.

That night, at the beginning of the reception, the father of the bride added two *more* (unscheduled) speakers while he was talking. *They* knew they were speaking, and they stepped up to the microphone with pages of notes, but I had not been alerted—and the very upset bride hadn't, either. The kitchen staff was also furious because they were now off on their timing.

One couple told me at our initial meeting that they had just bought a house down the street from the groom's mother and her husband. The bride described the house as "within leaping distance"—which turned out to be too close for comfort. The groom's mother had lots of opinions, which she voiced throughout the planning process. She didn't like the fact that the bridesmaids' dresses were black, and she was upset that her name wasn't on the invitation.

On the wedding day, I was with the bride at the couple's house early in the morning. I asked her how the rehearsal dinner had gone, and she confessed that it had been awful. She felt like her parents were treated as second-class citizens and that everything had been about the groom's mother keeping up appearances.

As we were talking, in walked the groom's mother herself. She had popped over from her house to get the groom's tuxedo and shoes. An hour later, she was back, looking for the groom's shampoo. This time, she saw that the women were having their makeup done and decided that she wanted hers done too. I had asked the bride and groom a number of times about the groom's mother's hair and makeup, and they had said, after consulting with her, that she would take care of it herself. I even noted that on the timeline. Now the makeup artist was in a panic. She was finishing the last bridesmaid but still had the bride to do, and then she had to get in her car and drive for an hour and a half to another wedding. She looked at her assistant, who was there to help but was not a makeup artist, and nicely asked her if she could do the groom's mother's makeup. The mother of the groom was thrilled.

Finally, everyone was perfectly made up and looking lovely, and the photographers arrived at the bride's house—but then the groom called and said his mother wanted photos taken at *her* house down the street, so the photographers left and never had a chance to photograph the bridesmaids, the bride's parents, or the bride getting ready. Sometimes, especially when you're planning a wedding, a little extra distance is a good thing.

At one wedding, the bride's sister—who was the maid of honor—gave a toast, defining love as "friendship on fire." And then she told the bride and groom to fuel it!

One bride and groom wanted to have a flower boy. To convince their little nephew to do it, they called him the Flower Jedi.

One groom's family was having 114 guests *versus* (that was the mother of the bride's word) the bride's 62. The bride's parents wanted to ask the groom's parents for money to pay for their guests at the reception. I was worried that the conversation could get ugly, but it didn't, and in the end, the groom's family contributed money toward the party.

One groom's sister had all kinds of personal issues and drama, and things escalated just weeks before the wedding. The family members were doing their best to include her, but I really felt for them and for the groom, who was forced to cope with all of this in the midst of planning what should have been a very happy occasion. Then the day before the wedding, the sister had a huge fight with the bride and her mother. The mother of the bride was late to the rehearsal and was so upset. I never heard the details, but, at the last minute, the groom's sister was nixed from the wedding party.

On the day before the wedding, the bride and groom confided to me that the groom's parents were "sort of separated," but said that no one was to know. The groom explained that his parents were from a different era and culture, and the instructions were that I should help take care of and protect his mother. "Cater to her," he said. The father was abroad until the day before the wedding and arrived just in time to walk down the aisle. Even so, the parents pretended that they were married throughout the entire event, and if you looked at this wedding from the outside, you would never have known. I was glad that the couple gave me a heads-up, though, as it is much easier to be on the lookout for a potential problem than to handle one after it appears.

I met with one bride-to-be, along with her fiancé and parents, for an initial face-to-face meeting, and the following day, she wrote me an e-mail apologizing for how she had treated her mother.

Here is an e-mail I received from one mother of the bride:

> *I realized this morning that we should set up a time for you and me and my husband to meet and go over things. I think we can focus on the timeline. This is basically so that he can buy into the whole production and not be overwhelmed with anxiety and start second-guessing everything on the day of the wedding. As a wife of 40 years, I know this is a wise and practical thing to do and will contribute to the smooth running of the day.*

One mother of the bride wrote to me:

> *I am glad you'll be there at the venue for our meeting. We may need you to sit between the Groom and the Father of the Bride and be a referee! We still have not spoken to the groom since he said some nasty things to my husband. Everything is great with us and our daughter, though.*

One mother of the bride commented to me right before the ceremony that she was very calm because she had gone on Zoloft about two months before the wedding.

When it came to choosing flowers, one bride e-mailed me:

> *I feel like the worst bride ever for not having a better feel for flowers. I know I want them in my colors and I am not really a roses kind of girl, but am clueless about everything else. How should I go about choosing a florist? I just want someone really good or my mother-in-law will frown on the whole night. If I am already talking like Bridezilla, forgive me!*

Another bride wrote:

> *One thing I did want to talk to you about is perhaps having someone to help keep my future mother-in-law away from me prior to the ceremony. She is very opinionated and I do not want her input while I get ready because she has already tried to push things that I am not interested in.*

One bride asked me, "Is there any way I can have someone watch how much our siblings are drinking? They drink a lot, and the last thing I want are sloppy family members at my wedding!"

Invitations can be a major source of family drama. One bride e-mailed me:

> *My mother has a problem with including my fiancé's parents' names on the invitation because 1) they are not contributing, and 2) she thinks the wording will be off because they are divorced. My fiancé and I feel strongly about including them, as they are important to us. But we are deadlocked, and I fear that this could spell the end of this wedding. Any advice?*

I responded, "Adding the groom's parents' names has become common, regardless of whether they are paying or not. It is certainly a warm and uniting gesture for all."

A few days later, she e-mailed back:

> *Thanks for your advice regarding the invitation wording. After a rather tense argument, we all agreed to include my fiancé's parents on the invite, as we had hoped.*

During the planning process, one couple told me that the groom's mother was not to know about the wedding and that they might need security if she showed up. On the wedding day, I asked them about this again and was told that his mother knew about it but wasn't coming— and happily, she didn't.

At one wedding, all three brothers of the groom gave a toast together. They went on and on and on. The father of the bride finally went to the caterer and asked to have dishes cleared immediately. It worked ... and the speeches stopped.

In an e-mail from one bride:

> *My mother doesn't think that the song we have chosen for our first dance should be our wedding song, and she wants us to change it. We will not because it has a lot of meaning for us and I wouldn't want anything else. Please do not tell her that I sent this email, it will only create a lot more stress and problems for us. We're just going to go ahead with our song and she'll have to live with it!*

The mother of the bride arrived on the day of the wedding with her own emergency kit and wanted to handle everything. She was bossy and demanding, and she even asked for water to be brought to the bridal party while they were on the front steps of the venue waiting for their photos to be taken. I went inside, and the caterer told me they would set up a drinks station in the lobby at the top of the stairs. I relayed this to the mother of the bride but it wasn't good enough. "*We need*

it here." So the venue and I brought pitchers of water and plastic glasses so that everyone could have water—and try to juggle pitchers and cups—during the photos.

I was in the hallway outside the ballroom with the bride and her mother, and the two of them were having a bit of an altercation. I spoke with the DJ after the wedding to find out what all the fuss was about, and he said that the mother had been insisting that he play the Electric Slide, which was on the bride and groom's do-not-play list. Both the mother and the bride were adamant, and the mother stormed off. Ultimately, the DJ listened to the bride and didn't play it.

One bride was very upset that her dog (a big chocolate lab) would not be allowed at the church or reception. She wrote to me:

> *I am DEFINITELY going to get a collar made from my extra dress fabric and take some pictures with her at my place. I would also like to have someone take her to the church to take pictures with us. Do you know how we can make this happen? My fiancé thinks I'm insane!*

And we made it happen.

One mother of the groom was especially high maintenance. It took her *forever* to have her makeup done, and I'm sure that it was because of her, not the makeup artist who I knew always adhered to the timeline. She finished with makeup about ten minutes before photos were to start and arrived downstairs about fifteen minutes late. I was already outside at that point, but she told me that she forgot to bring her flowers, as well as those of her mother and her daughter, so I went back upstairs to get them. Later, she wanted black safety pins to pin her bra and was miffed because she had to use my fashion tape instead.

A week or so before one wedding, I was cc'd on an e-mail from the bride to the caterer:

> *I have one painful but necessary request. There is a gentleman, the groom's cousin, at table 17 who will need a filet on a plate and literally nothing else. It should be well done to the point that the chef wants to cry. I mean burned to a crisp. If you can add some fries and bring them out on a separate plate, that would be great—but if not, just the filet and nothing else. Just a piece of meat on the plate by itself.*
>
> *I know that this is a strange request, but thankfully the cousin is a wonderful guy and it's a serious thing for him, so we want*

to honor it. Thank you so much for taking care of it.

I had been warned ahead of time about the bride's brother. He had been estranged from their other sister for years, but the bride wanted him in the wedding, and he agreed just days before the event. I was told that he might drink too much and end up shouting obscenities at his mother ... or worse. So when the brother grabbed the microphone at the reception, we all held our collective breath. But he gave a short toast to the best sister ever, and all was fine. Sometimes people do rise to the occasion.

At one wedding, the parents of the bride were supposed to see the ballroom right before the guests were invited in. I asked the bandleader if they would please play the parents' special song so they could have a private dance in the ballroom, and they did.

Four years later, I was with the same band and the same parents with their second daughter's wedding ... and I again asked the bandleader to play the same special song for a private dance. It was a sweet and lovely moment.

One mother of the bride contacted me and told me that she had booked a venue and a rabbi for her daughter's wedding, fifteen months away. The hitch? Her daughter was not engaged, and the groom didn't know about the plan!

At the ceremony, the mother of the groom (who was divorced) was set to walk down the aisle with the groom's grandfather. However, when the moment arrived, Grandpa was missing in action. At the last minute, we had to scramble to get a groomsman to walk the mother down the aisle. Then, as the ceremony progressed, we realized that one of the readers had gone to find Grandpa and was still missing—so we had to arrange for someone else to do the reading.

A week prior to the wedding, the mother of the groom realized that the last wedding director at the wedding venue would depart at four in the afternoon, but the party was supposed to go until five. She said that she didn't want to worry about guests leaving on the shuttles and could I or one of my assistants please stay later? Normally, the planner leaves after cake cutting, which is considered the last official act of the event, so I told her that per our contract, there would be an additional fee for overtime. So she told me ever so sweetly how much she enjoyed working with me and my team, and couldn't we just stay a little longer free of charge? So I called the caterer, who was having her staff handle the arrivals, and she said that her staff could handle the departures as well at no additional charge. Relieved, I e-mailed both the mother of the groom and the caterer so that everyone was on the same page. But a few days later, at the reception, the mother of the groom was still annoyed and went off in a huff when the wedding director left at her scheduled departure time—even though the event had gone beautifully and it was all taken care of.

One father of the groom had been in contact with the catering sales coordinator personally. She wrote to me, "He told me from the opening of our very first conversation that he was going to be a pain in my butt, and of course I laughed and told him it wasn't possible … but he is really trying to earn his title."

One mother of the groom had hired us for "day of" services, but it became pretty clear on the wedding day that the bride wasn't interested in our services at all. On our working timeline, it said that she and her new husband were supposed to go to the hotel roof for photos after the ceremony, but she never mentioned that she was going to have her hair restyled (from down to an updo) when she got back from the photos before the reception. Even her husband didn't know what was going on, but when I asked if I could do anything, and he gave me a definitive "No." I think there was a backstory here.

At one reception, I came across an elderly man who was lying across two chairs in the lobby adjacent to the party room. I didn't know if he was sick or drunk, but it was quite a sight, so I approached the father of the bride, who was attending to this man, and asked if we needed medical assistance. He said no, and that was that.

One mother of the bride came over to me during the cocktail reception and said that a cousin had brought her "baby daddy" who hadn't been invited. She was very upset, but I calmly I went over to the tent and requested that the caterer set another place at the cousin's table and serve another meal. It was an easy fix, even though feathers were ruffled.

From one bride to me right before the wedding:

> *One last thing that I've been wanting your advice about ... As you've probably seen by now, my mom wants everything involved with this wedding to be perfect and it tends to make me a little crazy from time to time. I'm worried that on my wedding day, she will spend time pointing out all the imperfections. It comes from a great place, but I really just don't want to think about or focus on what's not perfect. Do you have any suggestions for how to handle this? Maybe we can have a signal for when she starts worrying and making me*

*crazy? The other part of this is that I want her
to actually enjoy the day. Let me know if you
have any thoughts.*

I conferred with the bride and decided to hire two
additional assistants so that there would be four directors
(rather than the usual two) overseeing the event, and we
would have plenty of extra eyes, ears, hands, feet, and
brains on tap for the wedding day to keep an eye on the
mother and make sure that everything was executed as
flawlessly as possible.

One bride e-mailed me, "Do you have any recommenda-
tions for what to include in the wedding program? My
fiancé's sister is not in the wedding but it would be mean
a lot to his parents if she was listed in the program, although I'm not sure where/how to include her."

I replied, "It seems like mentioning his sister might
only highlight the fact that she isn't in the wedding. On
the timeline it says that the groomsmen are handing out
the programs, but perhaps you want to reconsider and
have her do this? Then you could list her as Program
Ambassador … or something like that!"

One bride wanted to know whether her future mother-
in-law had to be involved in the seating chart for the
reception. The bride knew that she had to assign the
guests to tables, but the question was really about *where*
the tables were situated in the space—and she knew

41

that her mother-in-law would have strong opinions and take offense if her guests were not given "good" tables. I replied, "One way to do this is to divide the room and have each family take approximately half, and then no one can argue because fair is fair. But sometimes that feels like there are two camps (like the Capulets and the Montagues!), so I usually recommend mixing up the tables if possible. One helpful trick: Often the tables are numbered with 1 being in the best location, but I like to suggest that a table in a far corner (and probably one that's less desirable) be table 1. This somehow makes those guests feel that they are still important. If they have a distant seat *and* they are at a table with a very high number, they may feel like they are not a part of the wedding at all." This solution worked.

With one family, there had been considerable discord throughout the planning process. There were conflicting religious preferences, and this became a huge and painful problem. But I must say that the groom's father truly seemed to understand fatherhood. He wrote to me:

> *Will I get through it and over it? Yes, I will do everything I can to do so, and afterward, the deep work will begin to heal myself and heal whatever needs mending with Bride and Groom, and I will work hard to be the best father, father-in-law, and grandfather I can be.*

And I thoroughly believed him.

3. *The Devil in the Details*

Planning and Logistics

*T*here are so many details, so many questions, and so many players involved in a wedding that it is imperative that a planner have a system in place for keeping everything straight. Especially since I never work on just one wedding at a time—I might have a dozen or two in different stages of planning all at once—my attention to detail has to be absolutely precise. There are so many moving pieces to keep track of. First, there are the people (the wedding party, relatives, and friends), where they need to be at what time, and how to move them from one place or activity to another. Then, of course, there are all the vendors and wedding professionals—the caterers, photographer, florists, and musicians—to coordinate. It's my job to make sure that they all understand their role in the wedding and have whatever they need (electricity? chairs? anything else?) to do what they need to do at the right moment. I keep everything straight by mapping it out on the wedding timeline, and I update each timeline at the end of every day with any new information that I've been given. This way, if I am hit by a bus, someone else will be able to step in and know exactly how the wedding is supposed to go.

Logistics may not be as fun or flashy as trying on gowns or doing tastings, but they deserve just as much focus because a successful wedding is all about the details. And in my experience, absolutely no detail can be overlooked. I once had twenty e-mail exchanges with a venue because the banquet manager had only allotted five minutes for the vendors to eat, a seemingly minor issue. But when I looked at the schedule, it was perfectly obvious to me that the photographer wouldn't be able to eat that fast and get back upstairs in time to capture cake cutting—and no cake photos would be a major oversight! The little logistical details of every wedding are important, and it takes a lot of effort and precision to make it all work. It really is a kind of staging and choreography.

When it comes to dealing with logistics, there are several types of client personalities. Some clients want to micromanage everything (early in my career, one wedding alone generated 1,302 e-mails—there were 82 one day, followed by 140 the next, and it was because of this that I finally gave in and bought a BlackBerry) while others are happy to totally cede control (for example, the mother of the bride who wrote, "I don't know what we want so I will leave it up to you. I will just pay the bills. You can ask me questions, but I would like you to do the rest. Is that okay?") Some clients are full of big ideas, but they don't think about how they will play out in real time. I once had a couple who wanted to have no less than *six* slideshows and videos presentations throughout the evening. I finally had to send them an e-mail in which I wrote:

> *I want you to have a fantastic party, but in my experience and opinion, six slideshows and videos will make the event seem more like a corporate dinner than a wedding. Think about it: You are asking your guests to sit in a darkened room and watch movies throughout the night. This means that there will be very little conversation going on, or at best, the guests' attention will be divided between the screens and each other. Please trust me that this will not enhance your guests' experience.*

Other clients try to manage logistics on their own, but they don't understand that even small changes or additions can create big problems if not handled correctly. I had one bride call me two days before the wedding and casually mention that she had ordered covers for the chairs at the reception venue herself. But how were these chair covers going to be delivered to the venue? And when? And who would put them on the chairs? And who would take them off and return them? She hadn't thought about any of this. Then she realized that she had also ordered chair pad covers—but not the pads themselves. When I pointed this out, she said that she would fill the cushions herself (150 of them because there were 150 guests) and then deliver them to the venue on the wedding day. I told her this was simply going to be impossible given everything else that was going on, so she finally found some willing friends to transport the chair and pad covers for her, and she paid the caterer to handle the rest. She didn't think it through, and as a result, she created a lot of extra work for other people.

A wedding planner isn't the smartest person in the universe—she or he just has more wedding experience than most. You've hired us, so when it comes to logistics, make it easy on yourself and trust us. When we recommend something—or even more importantly, ask you for some piece of information—it is not because we are nosy or bossy. We simply want to do our jobs as well as we can and make the day better, easier, smoother for our clients. That said, if you choose to do things your way, keep your sense of humor and be prepared for surprises. I had one couple who wanted a Tiki-themed wedding, and much to their parents' dismay, they insisted on using bamboo poles to hold up the chuppah. The mother of the bride e-mailed me a week before the wedding to say, "The bamboo poles weigh a ton. I can't wait until they fall on someone. I just hope it's the right people. I guess that's why we need a seating chart—ha ha!"

One bride e-mailed the venue on the Friday before her wedding to say that there were five wedding guests with food allergies and restrictions. These included a citrus allergy, a tree nut allergy, and a sesame seed allergy, as well as a guest with celiac disease (no wheat and gluten) and one who was vegan (no milk, cheese, or butter). However, the venue itself was not responsible for meals, since the couple had hired an outside caterer who was coming from New York City. The venue suggested—politely—that the bride would have to contact the caterer to have them provide special meals, sealed with guests' names on them for each course, which the caterer ultimately did, but it was a lot to ask on such short notice.

The week before the wedding, I sent the couple the final timeline. At 9:33 a.m. on the morning of the wedding, the groom e-mailed back, "Sorry, going through it now. Give me 10 minutes." We had been working on it for ages! They also neglected to forward it to their wedding party. Needless to say, there was lots of scrambling.

One mother of the bride mentioned during our initial meeting that she was thinking about making truffles for each guest. The bride pointed out that there would be 150 guests and that if she made two truffles for everyone, that meant 300 truffles that would all have to be put in boxes and wrapped. Her mother thought about it further and simply said, "Not all intentions are fulfilled."

I was overseeing my first Indian wedding, and I was excited but nervous. The baraat, the bridegroom's wedding procession, was going to begin around the corner from the venue. The groom was going to arrive on a magnificently adorned horse, and he and the groomsmen were supposed to walk over to the starting point about twenty minutes before the procession was going to start. However, when my assistant was leaving the hotel with the men, he looked around and found that they had suddenly disappeared. Turns out they had ducked into the hotel bar to have quick shots. They arrived on time, though, thanks to the prodding of the wedding director who spotted them and urged them to move along.

The bride's mother, on the other hand, wasn't at the venue when I had expected her. She had decided to stay behind and help the bride with her dress, but per my timeline, she was scheduled to be at the venue to perform specific ceremonial duties of welcome to the groom on the steps. She finally arrived *just* in time, as did the bride.

The weather forecast was for possible thunderstorms, and just as the mother of the bride finished performing her duties, we felt the first few intermittent raindrops. The timing could not have been more perfect. I had been worried about getting all the guests inside, and this cleared everyone off the steps and got them right inside for the reception.

Sometimes it's the couple who can't see eye to eye. I had one groom who was a Methodist but belonged to a fundamentalist church, which the bride described as crazy and "arm-waving." She wanted to get married by a judge, but he wanted to have (his) clergy. So then she decided she wanted to have a rabbi. She told me that it was getting ugly and that they'd had a huge fight the night before we met. Later, she told me they had compromised and that his clergy would perform the ceremony.

In addition, the groom had been married before and wanted all his children at the wedding, but the bride wanted adults only. Again, they "compromised" and decided that all the children would be there. The bride was so stressed by this whole situation, feeling that she was the only one who was compromising. She started calling the event a "big dinner" rather than a wedding to keep herself sane.

I met with one couple who was paying for their wedding and had a budget of $30,000. They wanted to have 120–130 guests, and by the time they contacted me, they had already booked the venue (which required an $18,000 minimum expenditure), and they wanted a particular band ($6,000). The bride wanted to hire me, which of course meant that they would have to pay my fee, and she went on to talk about how lighting was very important, as were the programs, and of course she wanted a florist, a photographer, an amazing dress, and so on. The worst part was that she later told me that they had taken out a loan of $25,000 and were using savings to cover their living expenses for the six months before the wedding. I knew that this wedding was *way* over budget, but the bride was not interested in cutting a single thing.

Later, she told me about the expensive jewelry that she had given to her bridesmaids as gifts. I figured that either she didn't tell me the truth about her budget or maybe her dad ultimately paid for part of it. If not, she is going to be in debt for a very long time.

The groom, who was in charge of most of the planning, apparently decided in the final few days before the wedding that he wanted to make some changes to the timeline, but the only one he told about them was the disc jockey ... so when the banquet manager, DJ, and I conferred on the day of the event, we found out that we had different instructions. We of course then worked together to make the evening flow properly.

One bride and potential client wrote to me:

> *As you know, we have been engaged since February this year. Shortly after our engagement, we unexpectedly became pregnant. This has caused us to rethink our wedding plans. We've since consolidated our*

households, sold his house, bought a new one, moved, are now nesting like banshees, and really wish to be legally married before the baby comes in early November.

I've spoken to the priest at my parish who has happily agreed to marry us on the anniversary of our commitment. Since I am as big as a house right now, I don't want to have anything too formal, but the church ceremony is important to us. In an effort to simplify this, we've agreed to limit the attendance of guests to parents only. I thought that we'd all go out to a nice formal dinner afterward.

My question to you is: What do you suggest that I do to make this ceremony more special? Any help would be greatly appreciated! I'm overwhelmed …

I responded:

For your ceremony, I would suggest that you have a bridal bouquet and that the groom has a boutonniere … and maybe flowers for your parents too. Flowers do make an event more festive. And, at the dinner, perhaps you want to have a personalized favor for each person. Although you may not be drinking, champagne is certainly festive … as is a special dessert. I would recommend a small wedding cake. And I would do the formal cake cutting (without squishing cake in each

*other's faces, but that's just my opinion!) And
I would definitely have a photographer there.
This is a big day, although it has a small
guest list.*

The bride was thrilled with these suggestions.

One bride and groom had ordered tables, chairs, and
linens from a tent company for their rehearsal dinner.
They had also ordered a tent to cover the outdoor
venue's courtyard, but it could be canceled three days
prior to the event without penalty … which is what
they inexplicably did. The forecast was for possible
thundershowers, and they canceled the tent! I sent them
an e-mail asking what the backup plan would be for 120
guests in the rain, and they e-mailed back:

*We are just going to roll the dice. I think the
only fear is that the heavens open up between
8 p.m. and 11 p.m. on Friday. We will have
to see how it looks Friday a.m. and if it is
planning on pouring all day, will figure
something out.*

This made me absolutely cringe, but amazingly, it
didn't rain.

On the Thursday afternoon before the wedding, the
groom sent an e-mail in which he wrote:

> *Attached is my guest list and proposed seating chart trying to optimize for all variables and solving none. Let me know if it works. I tried to keep family near us, kids either by the bar or dance floor and NYC randoms/family kiddie tables in the back.*

The bride responded:

> *I would not put the NYC randoms table in the 'cheap seats' at the back especially considering it is the weirdest table. We don't want them to be offended twice?*

One bride e-mailed me:

> *According to the groom's parents, who are paying for the décor, the limiting factor should be visual excessiveness or garishness—but not cost.*

One bride decided that she wanted to have water for her bridal party on the rented trolley on the way to the ceremony, but she said she didn't want to have to worry about bringing a cooler. She asked me if I could bring one, but I didn't own one. So I checked with the reception venue (where the bridal party was also getting ready), and with the trolley company, but they didn't have coolers, either.

The wedding drew closer, and the cooler issue kept bothering me because I like to tie up all the loose ends. Finally, I e-mailed the bride:

> *I am headed to Home Depot. Do you want me to pick up a cooler?*

The bride's response the next day (after, of course, I had gone to Home Depot and purchased several coolers):

> *Aw, so sweet! I actually have 2! I just didn't want to worry about yet another thing. I'll bring them to the hotel.*

I received this e-mail from a bride:

> *By the way, just to reiterate (And I have told the Maid of Honor numerous times) I DO NOT WANT A SURPRISE SHOWER. I want to look cute and I want to have input. I just wanted to bring this up b/c I feel like everyone always plans to have the shower be a surprise, and I want to nip that in the bud. :-)*

The bride and groom wanted their guests to sit on blankets for the outdoor ceremony, and the mother of the bride wanted *her* guests to sit on folding chairs. But there were only going to be 24 blankets and 150 chairs for 370 guests. I expressed my concern to the mother of the bride because I felt that a game of musical chairs could ensue, and I gently suggested that she should order some extra chairs and that the bride and groom obtain more blankets. And that's what happened. Everyone had their proper seats, and it was an amazing, joyous wedding.

From a mother of the bride, eight months before the wedding:

> *Is there an additional charge for you to attend the rehearsal? With 14 attendants, I think that it would be good for someone knowledgeable to be there to herd the masses (if you know what I mean). Am I an awful person if I am looking forward to this being over?*

She obviously didn't read our contract, because I always attend a wedding rehearsal.

One bride e-mailed me:

> *I'm getting a LOT of heat from some of my bridesmaids and mom about the timing for hair and makeup. My mom had initially said she wanted to go first, but now says she didn't know that first meant 9 a.m. and wants to go*

> *after I leave because she doesn't want to walk*
> *around in makeup all day.*

In short, in the interest of keeping everyone happy, we totally rearranged the schedule.

On the Tuesday before one wedding, the mother of the bride called and told me about all the changes she made to the transportation schedule without telling me. I was in a panic because I knew that the timing just wouldn't work. They had planned to use a trolley to shuttle guests from the church to the reception, but the trolley company had told me that each trip would take at least forty-five minutes, not fifteen, as the mother of the bride thought. The way she had worked it out, the guests might have to wait at the church for an hour and a half after the ceremony. And yet she was insistent that we use her timeline.

As it turned out, I was worried about the wrong thing. What I did *not* count on? The ceremony took about *ten* minutes. Yes, ten. I have *never* seen such a quick ceremony. Ever. So when it was over, we loaded the trolley (and I mean loaded, with standing room only, making accommodations at the last minute for two people with the altar flowers, one with the iPod setup that had been used for the recessional and was going to provide the dinner music at the hotel, and one very pregnant woman). We arrived at the venue at about a quarter to four in the afternoon. I called the hotel when we were on the way, but the hotel was, of course, not ready, as the cocktail reception was not scheduled to start until four thirty. The trolley went back to the church, and the final guests arrived at the hotel at 4:20 p.m. So I had been worried about late arrivals, when really I should have been worried about people arriving early! The guests had no choice but to wander around the hotel, and the hotel opened the cocktail reception about ten minutes early.

Before the ceremony, I went ahead to the church, and my assistant stayed behind with the bride, groom, and bridal party to make sure they got into the rented trolley. But when transportation arrived, two groomsmen were missing. They eventually showed up in time at the church, but no one could find them for quite a while.

For one outdoor wedding, the weather forecast said that there was a 40 percent chance of rain showers or thunderstorms throughout the day. That morning, I called the florist, caterer, and venue to see if any of them had buckets for umbrellas, and I asked the venue for a place for raincoats (answer: yes, up a flight of stairs, and we would need a coat check person, so I e-mailed the caterer to see if they could provide staff).

A bit later, I received a call from the venue suggesting that we make an executive decision about having a tent attendant stay during the early part of the night to ensure that the tent stayed in place as planned and to assist if the sides could be opened in clear weather or closed in inclement weather. Dinner tables were set in the tent, which was adjacent to the mansion. We decided to go ahead with this.

When the bride arrived at the wedding venue at a little after three o'clock, it was overcast and drizzling. We discussed the placement of the ceremony, and we thought it would probably have to be moved inside to the tent. She wanted to wait until five o'clock at the very last minute to make the decision. By five, the skies had cleared, and we set up chairs in front of the mansion—so all that last-minute scrambling and extra preparation was for nothing. But this was definitely a case where it was better to be safe than sorry.

One bride e-mailed her chosen venue, an art museum, a month before her wedding:

> *I just came back from the museum and wanted to let you know how heartbroken I was when I saw the exhibit. I understood when we signed the contract that there was a chance that there could be a nude or pictures of Jesus hanging. However, I would have appreciated you providing me some notice given the level of nudity present—I counted more than twenty paintings!—as well as the positioning of the crucifixion painting given how large it is and how it will greatly impact our event.*

Let's just say that all the nudes in question remained in the exhibit (it was an art museum, after all), but the crucifixion painting, which was positioned right behind the band, was draped off by the caterer, and it all worked out okay. The bride and groom had been afraid that the guests would think they had specifically chosen this exhibit, but even the bride admitted to me later that it ultimately made for a great story. And now, on every anniversary, their friends text them pictures of nude paintings!

One mother of the bride asked me to be the heavy on the day of the wedding and not let anyone but the bridal party into the bridal suite. One of the women from the groom's family, along with the groom's mother, knocked on the door, and they weren't too happy when I wouldn't let them in. But it turned out that they had a legitimate reason to seek out the bride and her mother: they wanted to know what time the family was supposed to be on the bus. I had given copies of the timeline to the mother of the bride at the rehearsal, and she was supposed to get them to rest of the family and the wedding party. So frustrating! How were they supposed to know where to be and when if no one told them?

I gave the women in the wedding party a fifteen-minute warning that it was time to get on the bus. Then I did it again at the five-minute mark. The bride was still in the makeup chair and was just about finished, but she still said that she didn't want to leave. Instead, she wanted to have her hoagie and not rush. This threw off the schedule we had worked so hard to plan, and it made everyone else have to wait around—but she was rude and did what she wanted, anyway.

When I first met one groom, he was extremely condescending, but he ultimately hired me for a large "package" of services, so I guess he thought I would be okay. The bride was living abroad at the time, and she and I had exchanged some productive e-mails. When she returned, however, she was really poor at returning e-mails and giving me information, even right up to the week before the wedding—especially regarding transportation. They had booked several trolleys, a double-decker bus, a Rolls-Royce, and two limousines to transport the wedding party and all the guests, and she never gave me lists of who was to go on each. I ended up hiring an extra assistant just to be on hand that day to organize transportation and make sure that everyone got to the right place at the right time.

Before one wedding, I received a frantic e-mail from one bride who told me that their food minimum was $25,000, but they were only at $22,781. She asked whether she could negotiate the $25,000 down or if they would have to upgrade to things they didn't want. I looked at the contract ... and saw that the minimum was $22,500, not $25,000! Couples, take note: it pays to read the contract. (One more good reason to hire a wedding planner—we're not attorneys, but we'll read the contracts and pull out the important details for you.)

During the cocktail hour, the groom pulled me aside in a panic because someone had dropped off a carton of eight bottles of "special" wine for the bridal party table—and he had no idea where it was. Of course, I located the wine and made sure it got to the right people.

For months, I kept asking for information from one bride and didn't get it. She told me in an e-mail that she had booked a limousine for 2:40 p.m. So, in caps, I wrote, "I DON'T KNOW ANYTHING ABOUT THIS ... we need to discuss transportation." Who was the limo for? Where was it going? And how was everyone else supposed to travel? Her reply was that capital letters gave her more stress.

From a prospective bride:

> *Thank you so much for meeting with me yesterday. I had a wonderful time getting to know you and I love the services you provide. I was all set to call you today to find out our next steps and sign your contract ... and then I was laid off this afternoon. So for now, I just don't know what will happen, and I can't afford to sign any new contracts. I need to see if I can find a job with a comparable*

> *salary first, and I hope I can make something*
> *happen fast and then give you a call because*
> *I really want you to be the one who helps me*
> *with our wedding … and I definitely need*
> *the help!*

But the story had a happy ending, because she found a job and ended up hiring me for the wedding weekend.

As I was driving to the venue on the Thursday before a Saturday wedding, I had a frantic call from the bride. She said that she had heard from the venue's managing director. When we had made a site visit to the venue—a public space—a few months earlier, we were told that a new statue would be coming to the center of the garden and that the bridal party would have to walk around it. We said okay and adjusted and adapted the aisle to go around it slightly.

But now the statue had arrived, and it was a seated nude woman … a very graphic seated nude. And, to make matters worse, it was huge. The manager also said that the green carpet that we had chosen for the aisle was green *plastic*, and she thought it looked horrible.

Fortunately, the venue had someone on staff with the equipment to move the statue while keeping the base, and I alerted the florist that it would need major decoration on top. I spoke to the tent company and rush-ordered a new white carpet for the aisle. They worked magic and had it brought quickly. Whew!

One bride did not want to assign her guests to particular tables. I tried to urge her to do so, as it can be confusing for people to rush into a room and try to find a seat … and then, if you can't find a place, you end up at a table of strangers. I suggested that the bride and her mother at least try it on paper.

This was is the bride's response:

> *I understand the problems involved in not having a seating chart. Let me explain why I don't want to do it. I've been to two events—one of which was my bat mitzvah—where not having a seating arrangement turned out to be advantageous. People who didn't know each other sat together and had a wonderful time, and we never would have thought to put them at the same table. People who we would have sat together were tired of each other and were happy to switch up and sit with someone new. I've also been to events where I knew that I wasn't welcome because the bride sat me at the 'reject table.' I am loath to make anyone feel like that (even that bride, who is invited!).*

We had further discussion—lots of it. I explained that finding a seat could turn into a game of musical chairs and how that wouldn't be fun for the guests and would waste time besides. In the end, they assigned seats.

During dessert and dancing, the groom's sister asked me if the trolleys were taking guests home, as her elderly grandmother was ready to leave. My timeline (which had obviously been approved by the bride and groom) said that the guests were going to find their own way home, and, upon request, I had listed some taxi company phone numbers on the timeline. I didn't know a thing about a trolley. No one had mentioned it to me, and I had no information. I went and asked security, and indeed there was one parked outside the front gate. When I returned to tell the groom's sister, she and the grandmother were nowhere to be found. I assume they took the trolley home, but it was all just so odd, and I didn't know what to make of the whole thing.

One bride told me that she had twenty tables, but when I counted, her table count had twenty-seven.

One florist e-mailed me at wit's end:

> *I have to say I am just dumbfounded. I have had more meetings and more communications with this mother of the bride than any other client, ever. For a request for a change in flowers to come in at the 11th hour—a week before the wedding—makes me very nervous. I am still trying to get her to give me final answers on items in my proposal that she has not yet confirmed. I explained to her in my*

last email that I am going to create a final contract and NEED confirmation asap in order to move forward.

This particular mother kept changing her mind on so many things right up until just days before the wedding, and she was very lucky that she had chosen such a flexible and accommodating florist. Fortunately, the florist persevered and did a spectacular job, and the mother was thrilled.

One bride and groom wanted a receiving line, but I tried to talk them out of it. "If it takes thirty seconds for each handshake and you multiply that by the number of guests, you can calculate how long you will be standing there. It won't be fun for you, and it certainly won't be fun for guest number 168 in line." So they thought about it and came up with a unique compromise.

After the ceremony, the bride and groom exited, had congratulatory hugs from the parents and the bridal party in the back of the church, and then the priest announced that the bride and groom would usher the people out of each pew. So they came back and personally greeted each row of guests. It was different, but it worked well; the process went much more quickly than a receiving line, and the guests loved having the few personal moments with the couple. Everyone accomplished the "thank you for coming" and "how lovely you look" conversations before they even left the church. Then at the reception, everyone could have fun dancing … most importantly the bride and groom.

I met with one bride two weeks before the wedding, and everything was fairly organized except that she had procrastinated about doing the wedding programs. Long story short, the bride was at Kinko's the morning of the rehearsal, and her mother-in-law-to-be hadn't finished putting the ribbons on them by the time we had the rehearsal that evening, so the groom had to bring them to the ceremony with him the following day.

The week of the wedding, the reception venue e-mailed me and said that the bride and groom had added a soup course. I think this was because they were under their guaranteed number of guests and were trying to make the most of their minimum. But if they had asked me, I would not have suggested adding it. They now had a salad, a soup, an intermezzo, and an entrée, and they really didn't need another course to keep people seated at the table and interfere with dancing and getting the party started.

One wedding in downtown Philadelphia faced some serious complications when I learned that there was to be a Jay-Z concert held on the Parkway—the major downtown thoroughfare—the same weekend. That meant street closings and big, potentially unruly crowds. In addition, many guests were expected to drive down from New York City, which meant more cars on the road and more nightmares in terms of parking.

I knew I needed a full plan of attack, so weeks before the wedding, I checked with the police department *and* the traffic police department *and* the Streets Department / Highway Division / Right-of-Way Unit to get the definitive word on street closures. I even contacted the executive director of the Parkway Council Foundation and the Philadelphia Parks and Recreation Department and Office of Special Events just to be safe. Then I came up with available alternate routes for the bus and limo drivers, and I added a bigger time buffer than usual for transportation, just in case. I also tried to make sure that the guests were prepared for street closings and/or traffic delays ahead of time. We put this information in hotel gift bags for guests and also suggested that everyone have a copy of the wedding invitation with them. That way, the police could see that the guests were on their way to the venue. We had copies for the bus and limo drivers too. Sometimes it helps if the police know that there is going to be a wedding.

All our advance planning helped, and happily, the wedding transportation went like clockwork.

When we heard there was a possibility of rain, I tried everything I could think of to encourage one mother of the bride to implement a rain plan with a covered walkway, but she wanted to give the guests umbrellas instead. This meant that we would need a few hundred umbrellas as well as a place to store them all at the wedding both before and after they were used.

Fortunately, the wedding day turned out to be glorious with not a drop of rain to be found. In fact, some of the guests used some of the umbrellas to shield them from the sun.

After each wedding, I always send out a questionnaire that asks the client to provide feedback about our performance. One mother of the bride said that she didn't think she should have chosen the "Unlimited Hours" package after all. I responded:

> *I saw that you commented that you weren't fussy and that you probably didn't need the Unlimited Hours after all. However, let me assure you that there were many, many, many, many hours spent on the planning and coordinating of your details. Since you were out of town and did not participate in this process, I did all the legwork with the venue and also the florist, which entailed a number of trips, emails, and conversations. And then of course there were the many details with all your wedding vendors to sort out. Even the small things—like the menu cards—took time. Your event seemed flawless and easy, I think, because of all the details that we attended to prior to the event.*
>
> *For a planner, it's not only about the end product but the planning, checking, and creativity that need to happen along the way.*

> *Clearly the savings that you achieved—on travel, calls, and site visits—were extensive. Costly and unnecessary mistakes and expenses were avoided. I truly hope that you were happy with the results and understand that the Unlimited Hours contract permitted me to pursue every last detail.*

E-mail response from the mother of the bride:

> *I hope you weren't upset that I answered the question that way. I know the wedding was great and it was because of your planning. I just wanted to make sure that we'd gotten our money's worth.*

The makeup artist called me two days before the wedding and said that she would arrive on Saturday at nine in the morning at Fourth and Market Streets. I had told her we would be at Seventeenth and Locust Streets. And this was after the bride had been trying to call her for a few weeks with no response!

On the day of one wedding, I was asked to put place cards at every seat for the reception. It was not easy, though, because, although the cards had been grouped by table, the order of the cards I was given was not the order on the seating chart. So putting them in their proper places took *way* longer than I anticipated. Also, two couples had canceled at the last minute, so a table of four and a table of six had to be combined. We couldn't do anything about the escort cards at this late hour, so we just put two table numbers on that particular table.

Once when I checked the ballroom right before the reception, I noticed eight huge bags full of dirty linens sitting in a corner of the room! I requested that these be moved immediately, and they were.

It had rained in the morning on the day of the wedding, and the forecast was for clearing skies, but it was still dark. The wedding ceremony was supposed to be outside under some gorgeous willow trees. The bride came to me and asked what I thought. I asked her if she was an optimist. She said yes. I said that I was too and that I thought we should set the chairs on the grass under the willows and near the waterfall as originally planned. I told this to the caterer, and we all held our breath and set them up … and we were right. (And lucky.) The sun came out just in time.

I once had to e-mail the baker:

> *I suggest that you talk to the caterer about*
> *serving the cake, since you mentioned that*
> *the cake serves 130 and there are some 150*

> *guests. The cake is the only dessert, except for a luncheon-sized plate with cookies on each table.*

They ended up cutting the cake into the smallest slices possible, and rather than dropping cake off at every place setting, the servers asked if the guests wanted it.

Once I went to check table settings with the count that the father of the bride had given me in the morning. There were five tables with more guests than we had thought. I went to the banquet captain and alerted him, along with the coordinator from the caterer, so that they could prepare the extra meals. Then I went to the mother of the bride and showed her. She said that her husband couldn't get anything right and that he had given me the original, full guest list and of course not everyone was coming or coming with a guest. So after all that work, we had to put everything back the way it was.

One couple called to tell me that they had narrowed down their venue search … to New Jersey, Pennsylvania, Massachusetts, Maryland, New York, and Connecticut! I told them I could help them once they settled on a state—but not before.

At the rehearsal, the bride casually mentioned to me that there were twenty-one vegetarian meals needed for the wedding dinner the next night. I have no idea why she hadn't said anything or why the venue didn't ask before. I immediately called the venue and told them what was required, but it was a close call.

One family was so lackadaisical about details that on the wedding day, they completely forgot about everything that was left on the to-do list. There were bags all around the getting-ready room, and I had to ask what each was to see if there were something I needed to do with the contents. That's how I found out about the glassware and sand for the sand ceremony (I took this to the ceremony site and assembled), cake boxes for the cupcake favors (I took them and placed them under the cake table), escort cards, family photos, and programs (which I put on each seat for ceremony). Turns out there was plenty for me to do, so I was very glad that I had asked.

The weather forecast was for ninety-four-degree heat, and the wedding was to take place outside. On the way to the wedding, I stopped at a dollar store and bought washcloths to put in a bucket of ice so the guests could refresh themselves between the two ceremonies. Yes, there were two. First there was a Hindu ceremony, after which the bridal party would change clothes while the guests had a cold drink outside, and then there was the

Christian ceremony. My intern folded approximately one hundred washcloths, got a container and ice for them (and another container for the used ones), and set it all up.

For one wedding, I spent hours and hours trying to determine what and how much transportation to provide. Guests were staying in room blocks at five different hotels. We of course had the lists from each of these hotels, but the bride insisted that a lot of guests wouldn't be staying in any of them and that other guests were there but not included on the room block lists. In addition, some guests would be arriving by train on the day of the wedding from New York City, so we went back and forth about how to best handle everything for months. Ultimately, we decided to hire a "transportation concierge," a wedding director who would walk between the three hotels that were in proximity to one another and manage transportation for the guests there, individual wedding directors at the other two hotels who would oversee the transportation for those guests, and two "sweep" vans to go around all the hotels at the end to make sure there were no guests left behind. It took a lot of logistical effort and coordination, but in the end, all went according to plan.

From a bride who booked the venue before she hired me:

> *I agree that we should provide as much seating as possible, but I don't think we can manage a seat for each person at the venue. My fiancé and I do feel a bit duped into agreeing to a venue that is too small for our guest list. Although we knew when we booked that we were on the large size of what they can hold, I was surprised to see that the floor plan only fit 124 (WITH the additional tent.) As we have already paid $3500 for this additional tent that we were not expecting to need when we booked, we're hesitant to double the size of the tent, because we got a quote and it would double the cost of the rental. Helpfully, we are receiving more "no" responses to our invitation than anticipated, so our maximum head count continues to drop. Right now I believe our maximum count is around 235.*

The final guest count was 184, but it was a beautiful day, so the guests didn't have to be totally enclosed, and everything worked out fine.

One client was planning a June outdoor wedding with almost four hundred guests plus all the wedding professionals (including the catering staff) … and yet there were only two available bathrooms, which were on the main floor of an old, adjacent building. I suggested to the mother of the bride more than once that she should have bathroom trailers brought on-site, but she resisted.

Finally, a few weeks before the wedding in an e-mail between me, the mom, and the caterer, I wrote:

> *I just want to register my concern again (for the last time, I promise!) about the bathroom situation. We have two bathrooms for almost 400 guests. This means you may have VERY long lines, so you might want to consider this again …*

The caterer chimed in:

> *We are expressing concern as well. In addition to the 380 guests, there will be upward of 80 staff on site for the day, including catering staff and other vendors. Lines will be an issue, but more importantly, can the existing facilities handle use by approximately 460 people? If either of the toilets become out of order we will really be in trouble. Perhaps a couple of functional johns could be placed in a discreet area for use by vendors, and then be made available for guests should the house rest rooms be over capacity?*

When she focused on the issue, the mother reconsidered, and the tent company had to scramble to find a suitable bathroom trailer. It was placed to the side of the building behind some trees and was unobtrusive yet available. Mission accomplished!

As always, I followed up with all the wedding professionals in the weeks before the wedding. The subject of the e-mail: I DO Wedding Consulting for Wedding on July 21. The body of my e-mail said:

> *Attached please find the preliminary (almost final) timeline for this wedding. I request your additions/corrections/comments so that this can be finalized.*

The response from the audio-visual rental company:

> *We have her wedding scheduled for the 28th.*

Glad I checked!

On one wedding day, I arrived at the bride's hotel room, and she told me that she wanted to rearrange the processional list as well as the recessional list and the list of introductions into the reception. I scribbled all of this down on paper and went downstairs to the business center to type out the lists for the bride, myself, and for the band. Fortunately, despite the last-minute changes, everything worked out fine. I asked the bride to look it all over right before she started, and she said it was just the way she wanted it.

4. Go Team!

Working with Wedding Professionals

In my previous life as a home builder and real estate developer, I knew that it took a huge team of people to build a house. I always used to say that we were like the legs of a stool, and if we weren't all there doing our part, the stool couldn't stand. Wedding planning is incredibly similar. It takes a host of people to create a day that will be an important, lifelong memory for the couple and their families and friends. Some of these wedding professionals—such as florists, caterers, and photographers—are the obvious ones, because they are hired separately and by contract. But the others—the servers, delivery staff, and the like—are the hidden talents that help the day go smoothly. The reality, of course, is that the planner helps coordinate the entire team and serves as the "coach." And a coach is only as good as the players, all of whom need to be working together. I once planned a wedding where the on-site caterer was in charge of some things (food service; table, chairs, and chair covers; dishes and glassware; serving and personal utensils; and barware and bar service), the florist was in charge of others (decor, linens, centerpieces, personal flowers, and putting the menus from the off-premises Indian caterer into the napkin folds), and the off-premises caterer yet others (food delivery, preparation, and plating). And it was my job to coordinate all of them. We held a finalization meeting that felt more like a global summit to help everyone understand the details and pin down their responsibilities.

Over the years, I have worked with many amazing, dedicated, caring, and talented wedding professionals who take pride in their craft and the job they do. Having said that, there have also been times when I raised my eyebrows and muttered under my breath, "Come on, guys, whatever happened to teamwork?" No matter how simple or elaborate the wedding, and no matter how much a family has chosen to spend, every couple has the right to expect that their wedding professionals will do their best work *and* work effectively—and peacefully—with everyone involved.

To give you a sense of just how complicated the behind-the-scenes work at some of these weddings can be, here is a list of the preparations that took place in the week leading up to one Saturday wedding—an outdoor, tented affair with an elegant, country chic atmosphere. The florist ended up being "captain" of the installation, for which I was grateful. Note that the work outlined here was *just* for the decor and related items, which will give you a sense of just how many professionals might actually be involved in a wedding setup, to say nothing of the rest who appear and work hard on the actual day of the event:

Monday:
◊   Tents, ceiling liners, and subflooring installed

Tuesday:
 ◊ Generators delivered

Wednesday:
 ◊ Chandeliers arrived and hung
 ◊ Nursery plantings delivered for around porta-potties
 ◊ Light check
 ◊ Napkins delivered to florist

Thursday:
 ◊ Carpet, stage, and dance floor installed
 ◊ Florist does draping along the back wall of tent
 ◊ Porta-potties delivered

Friday:
 ◊ Rentals for the caterer arrive
 ◊ Caterer sets up round dinner tables, head tables, bars, service
 ◊ Farm tables delivered and set up
 ◊ New landscaping planted

Saturday:
 ◊ Florist decorates at church and at hosts' home
 ◊ Cocktail tables and chairs set
 ◊ Cocktail table linens and arrangements, round dinner table linens, head table linens and runner, and farm table linens and runners all set by florist
 ◊ Farm table chandeliers decorated
 ◊ Round dinner table elaborate centerpieces—twenty-four in total—set
 ◊ Wedding party flowers delivered

◊ Catering staff sets dinner place settings and napkins at round tables, head table, and farm tables

◊ Florist sets place setting detail (a peony at each napkin)

◊ Escort card table decor set with escort cards, sign-in frame, book, and pens

◊ Placed Solemates (plastic tips to put on high heels so they don't sink into the grass) in glass bowls and the contribution frame (the bride and groom were giving a contribution to a favorite charity in honor of their guests in lieu of favors, and a sign was framed) on a table outside the back door so all could see them

◊ Coffee table arrangements and other house arrangements set

◊ Caterer sets dinner chairs

◊ Church urns placed near tent after ceremony

◊ Florist places twenty lanterns and votive stakes and a shepherd hook with a sign on the driveway

◊ Wedding cake decorated with peonies

Saturday night/Sunday:
◊ Breakdown by florist, caterer, lighting

Monday:
◊ Vendor arrives to collect farm tables
◊ Caterer collects other rentals
◊ Nursery breaks down plantings
◊ Tent company breaks down tents

In my experience, the best wedding professionals know their roles *and* mine and take the time to discuss the wedding well in advance. We stay in touch with each other throughout the planning process, and the key is clear, frequent, and responsive communication. Professionals: If you don't play well with the group, please know that a planner will have trouble recommending you for their next wedding. By the same token, please don't think that your work is overlooked. I am forever grateful to all the amazing professionals I get to work with who are so good at their individual jobs and who understand the nature and value of teamwork. I am always appreciative of not just the "big picture" efforts but also of the small details that help make the day a success. After one particularly challenging wedding, I sent the following e-mail to the venue and the caterer:

> *I am writing to you because once again I witnessed amazing teamwork last night, and I wanted to tell you how just much I appreciate working with everyone at your venue. All of the details, including the obvious ones like getting the building open, making sure that the wedding professionals were loaded in (and fed!), getting the bridal party set and down the aisle, and coordinating dinner with the kitchen and the band, were as always handled with professionalism, attention, and care. But it was the other things, like setting up pill bottles as escort cards which were not in alphabetical order, to delivering pitchers of ice water when the bridal party demanded it, to cleaning up the getting-ready area after it*

was left a mess, to putting flowers decoratively on the cake that was bare, to pitching in and helping to plate the meals, to personally serving pasta to two little girls, to putting empty flower vases on the dinner tables for the bridesmaids' bouquets, to getting up from a desk and swiping a card to make sure we can get to the second floor from the first, that were far beyond the call of duty. I just wanted you to know that I noticed how all of these things and more were done quickly, quietly, efficiently, and, most of all, with a smile.

So I want to offer a huge thank-you to all the professionals with whom I work. It is wonderful to work alongside you as part of a team! As you will see, there are sometimes challenges, and these challenges make me appreciate the best of you even more.

Before one wedding, I went to check on the ballroom, and I noticed that the wedding cake seemed to be listing slightly. As time went on, it seemed to list more, and I kept watching it and feeling nervous. Before the guests entered, I mentioned this to the banquet captain, who put an upside-down plate under the front of the cake to make it more even. Even so, the cake continued to list all night, and I was so glad when the cake was finally cut and whisked away. Disaster averted. Baker, what happened?

I was at a wine-and-food-station wedding in a hip venue with stunning artwork everywhere. The caterer had planned on three plates per person (I'm not sure why, since there were five distinct dinner stations), and—surprise—they ran out of plates. The servers ended up running down to the lower level to wash them and then bring them back up. I found out after the wedding that there had also been an issue with the hot water … as in, there wasn't really enough to wash the dishes!

Before one reception, my assistant and I went to check the placement of both the high and low flower arrangements in the ballroom. I had been given a floor plan of where the bride wanted the highs and lows, but it was nothing like what we saw. The bride had sent a floor plan to the florist too, but he hadn't followed it. Fortunately, we had some time, so I gave him my copy of the floor plan, and he moved everything around.

One couple had chosen a fabulous and stunning venue for the reception, and I was excited to be working there for the first time. The bride, her mother, and I met with the head of banquets. He promised a lot but took no notes. To make an ugly, long story short: the banquet manager quit his job, leaving the bride (and his boss) high and dry; destroyed some of her decorative items (table numbers, sign-in book) and signage so they couldn't be used; included most of the flowers requested in the proposal without charging a fee as he was supposed to, so we got hit with additional costs on the back end; and, of course, left no notes or instructions for others to follow. Luckily for us, the woman who was hired in the manager's place turned out to be very competent and picked up the slack in the weeks before the wedding, and we all pulled together to make it a terrific celebration in the end.

A few days before one wedding, I heard from the florist:

> *The bride came in here today and dropped off tons of items, like her flip flops in a basket, sign-in book, reserved seat signs, ribbons for chairs, votives, lanterns and shepherd hooks, hand-made pillows, and more. I didn't realize how much there was going to be, but no worries. She also said that I had agreed to take it all down after the wedding, pack it up and bring it back to the studio. Our contract*

> *does not specify that. This means that my staff*
> *will need to stay on site longer to remove and*
> *then transport all the items. I did not have*
> *this planned budget-wise …*

The florist was forced to go back to the bride and discuss this with her, but the bride was angry, and there was no pleasing her. The florist sent her a small gift, but the bride was unrelenting, even though she hadn't read the contract. Note: a contract's a contract, no matter what you think you discussed. This is why we *all* sign contracts for every part of the wedding—so everyone knows what to expect.

A band with whom I work frequently sent *my* client a form offering her *their* wedding planning services. I e-mailed them and requested that this part of their contract be *omitted* whenever a planner is already involved.

The forecast for one wedding weekend predicted a torrential downpour. Only a few days before the event, I spent hours on the phone trying to find a photo location in case of rain. I don't know why (a) the photographer didn't do this and (b) he didn't care, but it fell to me, and I was determined. I called a popular hotel (all of their rooms were booked), the venue (which couldn't accommodate us because of union issues), and then another venue where I had worked before. The woman I knew there said that she was going to be there at four thirty in the afternoon that Saturday, anyway, and she generously agreed to make sure that the wedding party had their photos taken, so that became the backup plan.

After the ceremony, it was pouring, but I had three of my I DO umbrellas with me, and my assistant and I shuttled guests to their cars and the waiting buses. Then we escorted the bride and the rest of the wedding party to the waiting trolley. Off we all went, and when we got to the venue, I had to use my umbrellas again to get everyone else inside. I was *soaked*. My feet were squishing in my shoes, and my socks were completely soaked through. However, the photos were beautiful.

One bandleader announced from the dance floor that he had been doing this job for many years and that he typically did eighty to one hundred weddings per year … and that he had never had so much contact with a groom. It wasn't said in a funny way but rather a snide one—a jab at the bride. Ouch! He also didn't stick to the timeline we had worked out; I had to tell him what to play and when, and it was altogether a difficult evening. Afterward, the couple was upset. I spoke with the bandleader, and he told me how difficult the couple had been with him throughout the process, and he was miffed that the bride had ignored him all night. I found his behavior totally unprofessional; however, the rest of the band still played great music, and the guests had a fabulous time.

One transportation company did not return my calls or e-mails during the week before the wedding. They hadn't responded to the bride and groom, either, but finally the bride got them on the phone and then e-mailed them driving directions. But on the day of the wedding, nothing had been confirmed. I finally reached David in dispatch, and he was very helpful, but the transportation was all confused. He had it that they were to pick *up* at the wedding venue and drive to, um, let's see, the Marriott in Willow Grove, Pennsylvania? *Huh?* The pickup was at the Marriott in Mount Laurel, *New Jersey*, with drop-off at the venue in Pennsylvania. There were to be two limos and two buses.

Later in the evening, when the reception was winding down, the two buses and the small limo were there—but the ten-passenger limo for the bridal party was not. I called to make sure the driver was on his way, and he was, but the time he had for pickup was ten o'clock at night, even though we had asked for nine thirty. Fortunately, it all worked out in the end, but it was an unpleasant and frustrating process.

The flowers were supposed to arrive at the bride's parents' home at noon on the day of the wedding. When they weren't there, I called the florist … who said she thought they were supposed to be there at half past noon, even though I had sent her a clear timeline. Not only was she behind schedule, but there was also an accident on the bridge, and she didn't arrive with the flowers until after one o'clock. The bride and her bridesmaids were supposed to have photos taken on the beach (with their flowers), but this was impossible because the flowers weren't there. They arrived just in time for the ceremony, and the bridal party ended up having to take their pictures during the cocktail reception.

Three weeks before one wedding and following the finalization meeting at the venue, I received an e-mail from the mother of the bride:

> *I must be honest, I barely slept last night (not because of anything you did). We were very stressed out by the things we were hearing for the first time yesterday. But the most concerning of all was the banquet manager. She is absolutely nothing like the one we originally met with, and I am very distraught at the thought of having this event that we've planned for two years in her hands. The fact that she was 20 minutes late to our meeting started things off on the wrong foot. After all, I managed to take off of work and make a 45-minute drive into the city during rush hour traffic to be there on time. This gives all of us serious pause. It also seemed like she just sat there and waited for you to tell her how things would flow. Leaving the cupcake box on the table was another indicator (for us) of a lack of attention to detail.*

It wasn't until after we left that we realized the new banquet manager didn't tell us that she'd send a new contract and floor plan. I have developed an itemized list of things we will need her to do and that should be included in the revised contract, but this manager has left us feeling unnerved. We are paying this venue a lot of money and chose them partly because of the first manager we met. What should we do? And with all that being said, thank you for being so good at your job. I really do appreciate all your help and support.

As it turned out, this was easier to remedy than it might have appeared. We had another meeting with the banquet manager to make sure that all the parents' questions were answered, and the timeline that I submitted to her was *twenty-three pages* long. I made absolutely sure to include every single detail so there was no guesswork for anyone involved.

The harried florist finally arrived … and the bride hated her bouquet and those of the bridesmaids. I checked the order, and the bride had been very specific about what she wanted, but the order didn't match what had been designed. I called the florist and told him that we had a problem, but it was too late to do anything about it. Also, the centerpieces at the hotel were supposed to be all hot-pink flowers, but they were a mixture of hot- and light-pink instead. They were pretty but definitely not what the bride had ordered. The florist's defense: by adding the light-pink flowers, the hot pink ones stood out, but that's *not* what the bride had wanted.

Right before the guests were invited in to the reception, I was standing in the ballroom with the florist. All of a sudden, the florist told me to look at the bandstand. The band had used heavy electrical tape to tape their wires on the *front* of the bandstand where everyone could see them. It looked horrible and ridiculous. Amateurish. And this band was being paid a fortune! The florist asked if I wanted him to go and remove the tape, and I said yes. And he did, for which I was grateful.

At one wedding, the corsages for the mother of the bride, mother of the groom, and grandmother were supposed to be worn on their wrists, but when the corsages arrived, they only had pins. I e-mailed the florist frantically:

> *Mother of the bride, Mother of the Groom, and Grandmother were apparently supposed to have wrist corsages … Can you make the change when we get to the venue???*

The florist's reply:

> *Sorry Lynda, the staff chose poorly, instead of asking me.*

The florist should *definitely* have checked the order, or at least had someone make new corsages and bring them to the venue. But he insisted that he just couldn't make it happen, so all we could do was to pin on the corsages and go with it—but it worked.

On the day of the wedding, the personal flowers arrived for the bride and other women on time, but no flowers were delivered for the men. I called the florist, and she said they were at the church. I told her that they were supposed to be at the hotel, so she had her helper leave the church and bring them over to us. Unfortunately, they weren't there before the men had to leave for the ceremony, so I had to call back and ask that the flowers be kept at the church. Who's on first? However, our wedding director was in the lobby of the hotel and happened to see the florist's helper just as she arrived and managed to rush the flowers to the men who were already seated on the rented trolley. It was a comedy of errors, but everything seemed okay.

As it turned out, we weren't finished with flower drama. At the reception venue, the caterer and florist were setting up when I arrived. Everything seemed to be fine, but as it got closer to the time for the guests to finish cocktails, I walked into the ballroom. There were beautiful tapers on the tables with lovely centerpieces, some high and some low, but only a few tables had the tapers lit. The catering staff told me that they had lit the candles and, within ten minutes, the candles had dripped and burned down so fast that they feared that the flowers would burn too. Even on the tables with low centerpieces and separated candlesticks, the candles were dripping all over the cloths.

I called the florist again, and she said that her husband would pick up more candles and bring them to the venue. I made it clear that we needed dripless or battery-operated candles. We texted back and forth about this, but she said that this was the only type of candles that she used and that it was the best candle in the industry. I responded that the catering staff had said they could not be lit because they would drip all over the food.

The biggest problem now was that the room looked ridiculous with all these unlit candles. It looked like someone had forgotten to do their job. And, since we didn't want the guests to decide to light them themselves, I suggested that all the candles be removed and that only the votives remain on the tables.

The florist's husband finally arrived with his hands full of tapers, right before the guests were to enter the ballroom for dinner. He was miffed and wanted us to use them, but the venue, caterer, and I all agreed that it was too late to do anything, especially since these were the same kinds of candles that had caused the problem in the first place. So we opened the doors for guests without any tapers in the room.

The bride and her mother saw that there were no tapers from the doorway and were upset. I reassured them that they were the only ones that even knew there were supposed to be tapers, and I reminded them that there could be a fire hazard if the tapers were lit, so in the end, they were okay with the way things were— although I was sure they would have a tense conversation with the florist the following week.

The florist texted me again later that evening and said, "Thank you, and so sorry for the stress!" Actually, I appreciated that she reached out and recognized that it had been stressful for us all.

One mother of the bride sent me an e-mail about a list she had received from the photographer, who had instructed her that she needed "to remind the guests that they are not allowed to take pictures when the photographer is working." It also said, "any gratuities will be appreciated." Hmm ... exactly how did he want the mother to instruct her 350 guests? And I had *never* seen a formal request from a wedding professional for a gratuity. They are always appreciated, but they are never solicited, which I thought was poor form.

The bagpiper called me to say that he was stuck on the bridge on the way to the church. He was supposed to start at a quarter after two, but he arrived just before three, right before the bridal party arrived at the ceremony. It wasn't a huge deal, but late vendors are always nerve-racking for the planner, who doesn't want to see the couple and the families disappointed. And there is no plan B for a bagpiper if he doesn't show up! I was glad he did.

After the ceremony, everyone proceeded to the venue. The bride and groom, the bridal party, and guests all arrived … but there was no sign of the photographers or videographer. I still don't know what happened— did they get lost? Take a little break? Finally, the photographers arrived, and they immediately copped an attitude because the bride and groom were a bit frantic (for good reason). They had wanted to attend at least some of their cocktail reception and had lost probably a half hour waiting for the photographers to show up. We pushed dinner back by fifteen minutes, but it was still a rush to get the photos. And no apologies were offered from the wedding professionals at all—just attitude. It is hard to understand this kind of behavior, and needless to say, I never worked with them again.

The florist dropped the personal flowers (bouquets and boutonnieres) off at the hotel, and I checked them. All were there. But when the bride returned from the hairdresser, she saw the bouquets and hated them. The florist had added a row of greens around the bottom, and that was not the bride's vision at all. So I took a pair of scissors and cut off all the greens. Then the bride was concerned about the centerpieces. I had the bride call the florist directly, who e-mailed photos of what would be delivered this afternoon. The bride ended up having the florist redo the centerpieces at the last minute by removing the greens from them too.

At one reception, the candles on the dinner tables had lampshades, and several were *on fire* when guests entered the ballroom. Note to florists: *please* be careful about the air-conditioning and live flames!

I once oversaw a reception where the band was good … and excruciatingly loud. The groom was upset, as were many guests. I questioned the sound technician, and he said that he had been told that the room was nine thousand square feet, and he was blasting music for that space. I don't know about the size of the room, but the music was unbearable. Finally, after *several* of us spoke to him, he adjusted the volume.

One mother of the bride went into the ballroom while the bridal party was doing hair and makeup and came back to say that she *hated* the centerpieces. I went down to have a look and had to agree—they all included some random flower that looked like a weed, with yellow flowers and orange tips. It was a casual flower that just didn't belong in an arrangement filled with formal roses. I called the florist, and fortunately he sent someone out to remove the offending flowers.

At one reception, we had an issue with wine. The liquor vendor had advised that there would be 29 bottles of wine for dinner, half red and half white, but with 140

guests, they totally miscalculated and started running out of white at the beginning of the meal. With 140 guests, that only allowed for one glass of wine per person at the most. So the caterer sent someone out to a local liquor store at about nine forty-five (the store closed at ten) to pick up two *dozen* more bottles of white wine. The father of the bride was furious. We were told that lots of men had been drinking white wine during cocktails and that that was why it had run out early, but a year later, I had another bride who wanted to use this vendor, and he again suggested one glass of wine per person.

No live flames were permitted at the venue, so the mother of the bride had provided two battery-powered candlesticks that were to be used for the ceremony along with two batteries. However, it turned out that *each* candlestick needed two batteries. I asked security in the building where the nearest convenience store was, and she told me that there was one less than a block away. I literally ran there, bought the additional batteries, and ran back.

We had had several meetings at the venue where the caterer, venue manager, and I were all assembled together and went over the whole timeline. At one meeting, the caterer's assistant was there. I called the assistant on the day prior to the wedding and asked if we were okay with everything, and she said yes.

The caterer was supposed to deliver lunch for the bridal party on the wedding day at ten thirty, but at 10:40 a.m., when there was no lunch in sight, I called him. I reminded him that lunch was supposed to be delivered at ten thirty, and he said, "You wrote a beautiful timeline, but I didn't read it." *What?* It turns out that the assistant had handed him the timeline, but he forgot.

The day before the wedding, we discovered that the hotel conference room where the bride was scheduled to get ready with her bridesmaids had a leak in the ceiling, so they reassigned us to a room one floor above it. We discussed that the hotel would put notices in the bridesmaids' in-boxes/phones so they would know where to go, and I was assured that there would be employees on hand to direct everyone.

The next morning, I went up to check on the bridal party, and the bride told me that the hotel had put notices in *all* seventy-five reserved rooms that there would be a hospitality suite on the fifth floor. So one of the first things I did was to make a sign for the door that said Bridesmaids Only, Please.

At the reception venue during the cocktail hour, a photographer walked into the vendor area with a plateful of shrimp and crab claws for himself and another photographer. I told him that the cocktail reception was not for wedding professionals, and he was rude and clearly felt entitled. One of the band members also had a plate piled with shellfish, as did the videographer. I told the bandleader that it wasn't for us, and he supposedly went and told the rest of his band. This was standard protocol that any wedding professional should have known, but they still weren't happy. Ugh!

One maître d' that I worked with at a reception venue was a terrific guy. When the bride and I were meeting with him about ten days before the wedding, he suddenly received a call that his mother had had a medical problem and been declared dead but was then resuscitated. On the morning of the wedding, he called me to tell me that his mother had passed away that morning. Still, he said that he would be at the venue in the morning to check things out, and he then returned there at ten o'clock at night as things were winding down to make sure that everything had gone smoothly. He was one of a kind, and given difficult circumstances, he showed a truly amazing dedication to his job.

One couple had ordered a '62 Bentley to take them to and from their wedding ceremony. All the details were confirmed. When the day arrived, we were on a tight schedule, and, when the car wasn't at our hotel at two in the afternoon, I called the limousine company … and was told that the car was at the wrong hotel. The driver hastily came to us from where he was—fortunately just a few blocks away.

One photographer's new assistant approached me at the reception with business cards and asked where to put them. I told her that the vendors weren't supposed to display their business cards, but since these had the website where the evening's photos could be seen, I suggested that she put them in a pile on the bar. A bit later, I looked at one of the guest tables, and there was the photographer's business card at every place! I mentioned this to the photographer, and he said that his assistant was new and that she would pick up the cards. A little later, he told me that she had picked up about 75 cards—but *there were 352 guests*. So I went around the room myself, picking up the cards and putting them away.

One couple's photographer was nowhere to be found the week before the wedding. I e-mailed him a copy of the final timeline and requested that he send me any additions or corrections, and, if there were none, to let me know that he received it. No word. I called him. No word. The bride called him. No word. Two days before the wedding, the bride's father went to the photographer's house and knocked on the door to make sure he would be at the wedding.

The cocktail reception area was adjacent to the wedding space. Shortly after the ceremony, I saw the photographer and his assistant sitting at a cocktail table. I suggested that they take photos because it was a perfect time to get candid shots of the couple and their guests. I didn't pay much attention to the photographers after that, as I was doing other things … until I saw them standing around armed with plates of hors d'oeuvres. I reminded them that we were there as wedding professionals, not guests, and that they had work to do.

One bride—who had still not sent me a copy of any of the contracts for her wedding, which was in eight days—left me a voice mail message in a panic. She said that she had been looking at the catering contract, and it said that the caterer was only going to be there for two hours, even though the reception was scheduled to last for four. "Am I going to be serving drinks in my wedding dress?" she asked.

When I called her back, she said that it had been worked out and that the caterer had told her it was just a typo. He would be there for the full four hours plus prep time and cleanup. If she had just sent me her contracts, I could have handled it for her, and she would have avoided the panic.

According to our timeline, the band was supposed to start playing at 5:30 p.m. When I spoke to the bandleader, he said they would start at a quarter to six.

I said 5:30 p.m. But the band didn't start playing then, so they weren't playing as guests entered the room for dinner. Later, they deviated from the timeline again and skipped a whole dance set between courses, so the kitchen was less than happy. And then they took a break. As they went back to play, one musician guzzled a bottle of beer, and a singer took a water glass full of red wine and put it at her feet on the bandstand. This was the first (and hopefully the last) time that I will work with this band.

"I'm a candid photographer, so everything has to look natural," one photographer told me as she was posing the bridesmaids around the bride.

At one reception, the flowers were gorgeous, but the lighting was a nightmare. The pin spots—small targeted lights designed to highlight centerpieces (they are typically attached to ceilings or on high poles, and their slim lights are directed toward the top of a centerpiece)—were aimed too low, so the tables were lit like daylight. By the end of the evening, someone had turned off every single pin spot in the room, and it looked so much softer and lovelier. It turned out that the venue had moved the tables slightly, and the positioning of the pin spots was off, but we discovered this too late to do anything about it.

I had one bride who was adamant that all the posed family pictures be taken in the bridal suite before the wedding. The photographer e-mailed me, writing:

> *Have you ever heard of those cooking contests where the contestants are really limited to the food they can use—they might only have, say, a radish, an orange, and some rice—and they have to see how creative they can get with it? Shooting formal portraits in a bridal suite is the photography equivalent! And no one is ever happy with the result.*

Fortunately, the photographer understood the situation and was able to creatively do his job and, in the end, get beautiful photos.

One mother of the bride sent me an e-mail:

> *I met with the owner of the venue for one hour today. We covered three topics: Miscommunication (which is a nice way of talking about saying one thing and then saying something else), sloppiness about details (including previously quoted costs), and finally lateness and cancelled meetings.*

The venue representative definitely stepped up her game after this.

Once I was examining a catering contract and noted—with some alarm—the price for vendor meals. So I sent this e-mail to the caterer:

> *I know that the parents of the bride are eager to serve their vendors terrific meals. But I have NEVER seen vendor meals priced at $78 per person. I have had meals that cost the hosts $20, maybe $30 or $40, and sometimes I have actually been served the same meal as the guests WITHOUT the hosts paying extra—because we all know that there may be extra meals any time the guests are offered several choices. Vendor meals are meant to be a courtesy to the wedding professionals who provide their services for the weddings and are of course a gift from the host. But not a $78 gift!*
>
> *Neither my assistant nor I will accept a $78 vendor meal, so please count us out for the food.*

And this was for vegetable risotto! In the end, the caterer cut the price in half ... and we had risotto with lots of peas in it.

One of my assistants and I were sent to the employee cafeteria in a fancy downtown hotel for our vendor meal. The bride's parents had ordered boxed lunches, but instead, a big pan of baked beans with diced hot dogs in it was waiting for us. The band was there eating, so we had some too. As I was leaving, I saw the boxed lunches finally being brought in, but they had arrived too late for us to eat. All the wedding professionals had to get back to work in the ballroom by the time the food the parents had paid for arrived.

The florist told me that the baskets with flower petals for the flower girls would be held near the room where the ceremony was to take place. I don't know if they forgot to put the petals in or what happened, but we had to hold up the wedding procession for maybe ten minutes while we waited for those baskets to show up. We finally started without them, and they arrived just before the little girls began walking down the aisle.

Fourteen flower arrangements were ordered for the rehearsal dinner, but only nine were delivered. Since there were long rectangular tables, we spread the arrangements out evenly in the space. It looked okay, but there was definitely more room between arrangements than we'd expected. The florist had to admit the mistake, and the family only paid for the nine.

At one reception, the wedding cake developed a huge air bubble on top. It was a hot day, and the cake just reacted to the high temperature. The ceremony venue was an old house, and the reception was in a tent outside, so there wasn't enough cool air to protect it. There was a pair of porcelain birds that were to be the cake toppers, but we didn't add them until right before the cake was cut so that they wouldn't sink into the frosting.

In the weeks leading up to the wedding, the bride couldn't seem to get in touch with the bandleader. I called his home and cell and e-mailed him too, to no avail. Finally, we made contact, and it seemed that everything was okay. But what we didn't know until the day of the wedding was that the bandleader had been very ill. I think it was his intention to perform at the wedding, but he ultimately wasn't able to do so, so he sent the bandleader from another band, which we didn't know was happening until the moment he arrived.

One band refused to stick to the timeline. Grr. The party was to end at one thirty in the morning, but at a quarter to one, the band asked to take a break for dessert! *Dessert?* Since when does the band get a dessert break? The mother of the bride said *no* and told them they could break at a quarter after one—which they did, and then they played canned music until the end of the party. Outrageous. After the wedding, the bandleader had the nerve to ask me for a recommendation.

On the morning of the wedding, I went to the venue to start checking on ceremony details. When I arrived, I was told that the freight elevator—which held the chuppah components, some tables, band equipment, flowers, *and* two florists—was stuck between floors. This lasted for about an hour and a half, but eventually we got them all out.

One couple I worked with hired a band they had heard at a bar. On the day of the wedding, the bandleader came over to me during setup and said that he'd had a conversation with the banquet manager two weeks prior and that she told him he needed insurance coverage. He told her that he didn't have it. So now, on the wedding day, she didn't want the band to play because they hadn't provided an insurance certificate. The leader was frantic, called his insurance agent, and tried to get insurance about a half hour before guests were to arrive—but finally the manager relented, and the band played without having insurance in place.

Once there was a very tall and prominently placed glass tip jar on the bar at the cocktail reception. The banquet manager saw me taking a photo of it, and so she went over to the bar and removed it.

In a particularly frustrating experience with a transportation company, all was confirmed (twice), as recently as the day before. However, the bus company that the couple had hired (I had never heard of them—the bride knew them somehow) had apparently subcontracted the work to someone else, and the bus got lost and arrived an hour late.

One bride hired me *eight* weeks before her wedding and copied me on this e-mail to the hotel:

> *My fiancé called everyone last week because frankly, we have been extremely disappointed in the overall service by the (FANCY) Hotel so far. This past week we've had to explain to our guests that no, the wedding is not cancelled, because people keep calling for the room block and have been told that not only is there no room block (apparently our reservation didn't go through even though I hand-delivered the application to someone at the hotel's front desk), but also that no such wedding exists—even though you have tens of thousands of dollars of our money so far. I have been emailing/calling to make sure things are on track, but we feel that someone there needs to actually take charge, and give us some kind of guidance. This has been extremely disappointing and upsetting, and is not something I ever thought would happen at your hotel.*

I got involved, and we started having meetings with the hotel, and all the details were worked out in short order. This was one case where the wedding just seemed to fall through the hotel's cracks—but to its credit, the staff stepped up quickly and made it right.

At about a quarter after five, forty-five minutes before one outdoor wedding, I noticed that dark clouds were starting to roll in, and the wind was kicking up. I went to the head of facilities and catering to discuss what we should do. It would take about a half hour or more to move all the chairs inside. The facilities manager went to talk to the couple, and they decided to do it.

What I didn't know until much later was that the staff was diverted from catering duties to move the chairs. At the cocktail reception, the bride's father complained to me that guests were hungry and that not nearly enough hors d'oeuvres had been passed. Only then did the catering manager tell me that her staff had first had to move the chairs, then finish in the ballroom, and then finish the food—thus the cocktail reception had been compromised. The dad was not happy, but at least we were dry.

When one couple hired me, they had already chosen their venue. I looked at the contract and immediately had a ton of questions, not from a legal point of view but from the practical-wedding-planner point of view. The venue was an established bed and breakfast, and they were about to construct a barn and put up a tent for the season so that their hotel could become a sophisticated country-wedding venue. However, this was the first time this B and B had ever hosted a wedding on the premises, and it quickly became clear that they had very little idea about what they were doing.

When we all met with the venue manager and pushed for clarity, the couple felt like the venue was going back on things it had originally promised. First it was small things, like not telling them until after they signed that a "choice of two entrées" would only be possible if they wanted to obtain their guests' entrée choices ahead of time. Then they were told that the barn would "almost definitely" be ready for use at the time of the wedding because they were breaking ground in April, although given that this was a June wedding, it seemed like there was no way it could be ready in time. Then the confusion extended to issues like the cost of flowers (flowers were supposed to be included, but no one could really explain what that meant) and the size of the tent (which no one could define).

All these things just led to a lot of stress and a rising budget, and the couple decided to walk away from the contract. I supported their decision, as the venue just wasn't ready for prime time. They ended up at a spectacular farm nearby.

The caterer had been MIA for a month, and we were at four days and counting to the wedding. The bride sent another e-mail:

> *Hi, when will someone be able to speak with me about Saturday? We still have yet to finalize the menu and go over a number of questions that I have regarding layout and logistics as well as the final list of rentals. Please let me know when (day and time) so I can schedule accordingly.*

That night, I finally received an e-mail from the caterer:

> *I am now directing all my focus and attention toward this bride's wedding. I'll be talking to her this evening and will go over the timeline and all the other questions she might have. I will get back to you after this conversation at some point tomorrow. I thank you for your patience and understanding.*

It was a good thing that I had worked with this caterer before and knew the business was reputable. Otherwise, we would have made a move to pull the plug before the four-day mark! But no matter how busy a wedding professional is, I still can't excuse not returning e-mails or phone calls—that is always a red flag.

One florist got all mixed up. The mother of the groom's flowers were delivered to the father of the bride's house (they should have been delivered to the church), and the father of the bride's boutonniere was delivered to the church (when it should have been delivered to his house). Fortunately, the flowers for the altar and the centerpieces made it to the appropriate places on time.

For one wedding, I thought that the florist would be handling all the items for the ceremony, since this is what they usually do, but the week of the wedding, she told me that she wouldn't be doing it. So I took the programs, fans, glass and water for the rabbi, glass to break, wine, wine opener, kiddush cup, silk basket and petals for flower girl, and Reserved Seat signs and set them in their proper places at the ceremony site. I secured a small table to hold the ceremony's wine glasses and also put the vows on it. I helped arrange for someone to take the kiddush cup, programs, ketubah, and glass that the groom stepped on back to the reception venue. I am always happy to help out another professional, but I am surprised when vendors assume that they don't have to do things that others in their field do regularly.

On the timeline, I wrote as I always do if I am working with wedding professionals for the first time: ALCOHOL WILL NOT BE SERVED TO WEDDING PROFESSIONALS. The bandleader actually wrote back:

> *Oh, one other question: the timeline says, 'no alcohol for the wedding professionals.' Just wanted to see if there was any leeway for the*

Lynda Barness

> band members to be able to get a couple of
> beers, or if this is a firm thing?

Really?

At one wedding, there were two security guards hired by the venue to oversee the event. We had a cupcake tower on the first floor, and when all the guests went upstairs for their dinner, one of the guards went over to the table and reached for a cupcake. I was right there, so I stopped him and requested that he put it back. I told him that the cupcakes were for the guests and there were a certain number and no extras. That ended the discussion.

On my timeline, I requested armchairs for the hora from the venue. I asked about them again when I arrived at the venue on the day of the wedding and was told that there were no armchairs. So the venue used their regular banquet chairs, and the bride slipped *off* while she was held aloft! Fortunately, she was only stunned and not hurt.

One bride and groom hired both a band and a DJ (who was associated with the band) so they could alternate sets, but the DJ told the groom a week before the wedding that he had gotten another gig (for $200 more)

and wouldn't be coming, regardless of what was in their contract. At the last minute, we were forced to hire a replacement DJ with whom the band had never worked. Fortunately, all the professionals worked together, and I suspect that no one except the bride and groom knew the difference.

On the morning of one wedding, I arrived at the venue to check on how the preparations were coming along. The chair bows had been delivered and tied as planned—but the color was wrong. I called the vendor, and she said that the warehouse was two hours away and that they wouldn't be able to get the right ones to us and tie them on in time, even after I offered to tie the bows on with two of my assistants—and, since it was a Sunday, she said that she couldn't get in touch with other vendors. I was frustrated because someone from the vendor's company had to put them on the truck, the person on the truck was supposed to check them, and the people who tied them on should have known. The room looked fine, but the bride and groom were disappointed.

The bartenders were *not* supposed to take tips, but they did. When my assistant asked them to remove the tip jars, they did … and then put them out again. Grr.

At one point toward the end of dinner, one of the security men came over to me. He said that an older guy—about sixty years old—and a younger guy had approached him and asked where they could go to smoke weed. *Are you kidding me?* I looked over the security guard's shoulder, and at the far end of the porch, I saw the two guests passing something lit between them. I sent the guard over to ask them to stop, and fortunately, they did.

One videographer didn't respond when I e-mailed and called (and left a voice mail message) the week before the wedding. Finally on the wedding day, I contacted him on Facebook, and he told me that two of his guys would show up. Instead, three of them did. One videographer stationed himself *under* the chuppah so the parents of the groom couldn't stand in their proper places. Needless to say, we will *not* be working together again.

The bouquets for the bride and the bridesmaids were delivered in vases, but there was no water in them, so the flowers were on their way to drooping when they arrived. Despite our adding water as quickly as possible, they didn't hold up for the rest of the day. The boutonnieres were of several types, but they came with no tags or labels, and the ends of the flowers weren't wrapped, so they too were wilting. The mothers' corsages were the worst of all: they were wrapped with something that looked like a rubber band, and there was a separate satin ribbon that was supposed to tie them on. The flowers didn't stay up, and I ended up using fashion tape to tape the flowers onto the mother's wrist. So much for that particular florist!

The beading on the cake provided by the venue was awful; it was uneven and falling off on one side. It was a very simple and straightforward cake design, so there was really no excuse. At this point, there was nothing that could be done, so we hid the offending side and hoped for the best. Happily, the party was such as success that I'm not sure if the couple even noticed the cake during the celebration—so we just did a ceremonious cut, and then it was whisked away to be cut and served to guests.

The mother of the bride and her daughter had helped to design gorgeous, elaborate, laser-cut invitations with an amazing invitation specialist. There were a number of pieces in each—the invitation itself wrapped in an intricate laser-cut folder, an RSVP card, a reply envelope, and two other cards with additional details about transportation and a brunch the following day. Each one required careful assembly, and the mother and daughter were thrilled with their creation.

A few weeks before the wedding, the mother sent an e-mail to the stationer and copied me, expressing her disappointment that she had heard from several guests that there was a piece missing from their envelopes. The mother explained:

> *I'm really disappointed that we paid so much to have them stuffed professionally, and yet the quality control for counting each piece of such an important and expensive invitation was lost.*

The stationer apologized profusely, and I expect that he will be more careful in the future.

In the final days before one wedding, I sent an e-mail to the venue's caterer:

> *I had a good finalization meeting with the mother of the bride today. Did you know that there is a SURPRISE appearance by the Mummers (one of the fancy string bands that traditionally parade in Philadelphia on New Year's Day)? The bride and groom do NOT know! Apparently Fralinger's String Band is scheduled to arrive at 6:40 p.m., right after the toast by the Father of the Bride. So the whole timeline will obviously need to be revised. Would you please call me or just let me know of the revised timing for the first course, entree, and cake cutting?*

The caterer e-mailed me back:

> *Yes, I was aware of the Mummer surprise. The father of the bride and I have been discussing and I was under the impression that I was to not share this detail with anyone other than the bandleader. We have the 'real' time-line ready to go and I will share it with you on Saturday.*

I was stunned—she would give me the timeline *on the day of the wedding*? How could I do my job? And weren't we supposed to be working together?

The Wednesday before the wedding, the bride forwarded me an e-mail about the five thousand beverage napkins that we had ordered for the eight huge stations during the cocktail reception, with the thought that there would be some left over for the bride and groom. Believe it or not, some 1,350 napkins were damaged during the shipping process—and there were no leftovers.

Two weeks before the wedding, the cellist was having a some form of repetitive strain injury in her hand. Her doctor recommended complete rest, which meant that there was no musician for the ceremony. Fortunately, I was able to locate a harpist on very short notice, and all went well.

I had just completed a beautiful wedding and sent this e-mail to the photographer, who had put the images in an online gallery:

> *I just went through the gorgeous images from this wedding! I have actually finished writing the submission to Philadelphia Weddings and hope that I can have these images soon. I am leaving for a destination wedding on June 6 and won't return until the 16th of June and would love to submit this wedding before I go.*

The photographer's response was astonishing:

> *I'm sorry, but I must limit the number of photos you use to a maximum of five. I know this is not going to go over very well with you, but in my 50 years of experience (yes 50) I'm still waiting for a single wedding consultant to refer us, or for the photos that we have supplied to magazines to bring us one lead. Believe me, we have tried. I know, bad attitude.*

And so, I wrote back:

> *I urge you to go to my website, www.idoplan. com. There you will see lots and lots of images in the Gallery, and all of them give credit to the photographer. I value the work of the photographer highly and always give credit when I speak and in anything I write. And any magazine that accepts a submission also gives*

full credit. In my experience (and I recently had a wedding featured in Martha Stewart Weddings!), the magazines typically want 50 images from which to choose. I send these via Dropbox with the submission information that I write. I know that it is important to this bride to have her wedding submitted to Philadelphia Weddings. Furthermore, I do believe that we all work together. And in the spirit of that cooperation, I request more than five images. I hope you will reconsider and provide me with the images so that I can submit this wedding to the magazine and also post photos on the I DO website. You will be credited in both places.

The photographer's response:

Sorry, but I will not be able to provide any photos to you directly. If the Jewish Exponent newspaper *or any other publication for that matter requests photos, I will make the decision as to which photos and how many to provide. The rights of these images belong to us and are available for use at our discretion only.*

I have *never* experienced such rudeness from any wedding professional of any kind. I told the couple and their families that I could not continue to pursue the submission, which was sad for the bride and her family and the photographer, as well. I have yet to meet another photographer who refused to have his or her work submitted to a magazine.

At the last minute, the mother of the bride asked me about flowers for the cake table. The cake had a monogram, but she decided that she wanted some additional decoration around the base. When I got to the venue, I asked the catering sales manager if she had any extra flowers or petals, but she said no. There were, however, three extra boutonnieres, so my assistant and I pulled two apart and sprinkled the petals around the cake. We saved the last one for further emergencies.

The cocktail reception was in a room that was supposed to hold 220 people, but there were 320 guests. No one could move, and the noise level was unbearable. One of the most important wedding planning rules: *never* assume that some of your guests will not attend. I tell this to my clients all the time.

Cell phone reception was not great in one particular venue, which had thick walls and bulletproof windows. It was a mansion designed and built in the 1970s for someone famous, and while it had a fascinating history and provided a gorgeous setting for a wedding, it made communication a bit difficult for the wedding professionals. Without our cell phones to allow us to talk and text, we did a lot of running around.

We arrived at the church to find two wrist corsages marked Grandmother and two boutonnieres marked Grandfather. Well, there were no grandfathers at this wedding, and there were *three* grandmothers. So we gave the two wristlets to the grandmothers of the groom, and my assistant, who happens to be a member of a garden club, took the two boutonnieres and made one corsage out of it for the bride's grandmother. I called the florist after the fact and was told that the wrong flowers had been dropped off at the church and that they were actually meant for a wedding down the road.

Once I learned right before the wedding that the bride and groom had hired a videographer. They hadn't asked me for a recommendation, so they hired a fellow who showed up with an amateur-looking camera, and it was obvious to me that he was neither skilled nor particularly interested in creating a well-done video. He didn't follow the photographer to get any footage of the couple, and right before the reception started, he announced that he was having a problem with lighting. When the photographer saw the lights the videographer had put up in the ballroom, he freaked. He said that they were the type of lights that are used on highways! I talked to the videographer and told him he couldn't use them, after all. I would love to know how that video turned out.

The photo booth company arrived a half hour late with a ridiculously wrinkled sheet for a backdrop and proceeded to spend over three hours trying to get their system up and running. It was right in the room that all the guests had to walk through to get to their seats for dinner and was in the space where the dessert was set up, but fortunately, the venue brought out screens to hide the mess. There were wires everywhere; it was such a sloppy job, and they didn't have the booth open until after cake cutting. Despite all of this, two of the three attendants found time to sit down and have a vendor meal.

Two weeks before the wedding, the bandleader wasn't responding to my e-mails. His assistant finally e-mailed back and said he would contact me at the end of the week. He didn't. I e-mailed again. The next week I called, and the assistant said they were busy and would get to it the following week. The wedding was in *two* days! He finally called and asked that cake cutting be moved back so the band could take a break at the same time. We tweaked the timeline, and luckily, everything went smoothly on the day of the wedding.

One venue started breaking down the tables from the cocktail reception and sweeping up while the bridal party was still lined up there for its entry into the ballroom. Ugly.

The florist delivered the personal flowers to the bride's hotel room. I checked them, and all were there, but when the bride saw the flowers, she was very upset. There were four yellow calla lilies in her bouquet and two in the maid of honor's, and she had specifically requested no callas. She was in tears, so I called the florist, and we cut the heads off the offending callas. When the bride got to the ceremony venue, the florist was there ready to redo bouquets. She thought she had been doing a favor by adding the yellow callas, but when she realized her mistake, she rectified the situation quickly and professionally—which is what I like to see.

One mother of the bride hired a security company but never got any paperwork from them. The day before the wedding, I called them to confirm. The number was obviously a personal cell number, so I Googled the company and wrote this e-mail to the mother and to the caterer:

> *I feel odd writing this email, but here it is …*
> *I tried calling the security company to just*
> *confirm that they will be at your home tomorrow*
> *since I don't have any paperwork, and there*

> *was only a private voicemail box, so I went on Google to see if there was an office phone number. What came up is that this firm was charged with operating without a license. I honestly don't know what this means, and I don't know the company, but I didn't think I should keep this information to myself. So here it is … (sorry!)*

On the day of the wedding, the company arrived and did a good job.

Occasionally, I wind up with a client or clients who just aren't good at communicating. I e-mailed one mother of the bride and said:

> *I have been trying to reach you by email and phone. I would appreciate it very much if you would return my emails/call, as it is impossible to complete your wedding timeline without your input.*

I even sent her an e-mail with the clause from my contract (which sometimes becomes necessary with clients like this one) that says that the company is only able to fully perform its duties based on information provided from clients.

The next day, I e-mailed her and asked who would be in photographs. Her response:

> *I do not know who will be photographed. How the heck do I know? The bridal party and the parents I assume. The answers to your other questions are: I do not know, I do not know and I do not know.*

I forwarded this to the photographer. His reply to me:

> *I still have not heard from anyone connected with the wedding, which is very unusual. Most of our brides are very concerned about their photography. My biggest concern is any miscommunication with the bride's family, due to their lack of communication.*

A week later, he e-mailed me again:

> *I spoke with the bride's mother yesterday. The bride still won't return my phone calls, so I have stopped calling her. This is a first for me—most brides are the total opposite!*

Finally, the mother of the bride sent me an e-mail telling me that she didn't have time to give me the information I'd requested. Since the bride and her mother hadn't responded to the other wedding professionals, either, I called them all myself, and together we all worked out the timeline on our own.

I once sent out a Constant Contact greeting to all my clients that said, "Enjoy the Dog Days of Summer" and included some photos of dogs at weddings. I received a response from a recent father of the bride who said:

> *You left out a picture of our photographer …*
> *one of the biggest dogs I ever met.*

One gracious florist wrote to the couple the next day:

> *I spoke to Lynda this morning to see how the*
> *event turned out. She informed me that you*
> *were one wrist corsage short, I looked in my*
> *back cooler and there it was. I can't apologize*
> *enough for my mistake and will credit your*
> *amex account for all the corsages. I hope that*
> *in spite of these problems that you both had*
> *a wonderful evening, the room was truly*
> *stunning.*

The groom graciously responded:

> *That is really no problem. The event was*
> *fantastic!! And there were many comments*
> *on not only the beauty of the arrangement,*
> *but the uniqueness of my boutonniere! You*
> *did wonderfully. Many thanks!*

5. Say a Little Prayer for Me

Clergy, Officiants, and Their Helpers

Some of the biggest surprises I've had at weddings have come from the people who officiate the wonderful, meaningful ceremonies that begin so many marriages. This is in part because we always expect officiants and clergy to be absolutely perfect, and when they don't perform as planned, everyone takes note. I have worked with some fabulous, caring, and sensitive officiants, but they are only human, just like anyone else.

One bride I worked with had problems with the priest throughout the planning process. There was a set of big, wooden double doors at the back of the church, and she wanted to walk through them and make a grand entrance, but the priest insisted that she enter the church through the side doors, make her way to the center aisle, and then walk down. He also didn't want her to wait outside in the limo and said that she had to wait downstairs. He would come downstairs five minutes before the ceremony to line everyone up (I could have done this, but apparently, I was invisible).

He also insisted that he would tell the congregation to rise as the bridesmaids processed down the aisle—but the bride wanted everyone to stay seated until *she* came down the aisle, which is the usual tradition. She thought about just doing what she wanted, anyway, but she was afraid that the priest would say something bad or make a remark about it during the homily. She was very upset about the whole situation. What was up with this priest?

On the wedding day, the priest was at the back of the church with the bridal party, and then he made his way to the altar, and the procession started. Although he'd said that he would ask the congregation to rise when the bridesmaids entered, as luck would have it, he wasn't at the altar in time to do it—either that or he just forgot—so the guests sat while the bridesmaids came down the aisle and then rose for the bride's entrance, just as she had wanted.

Some months later, I did another wedding at this same church, so I was ready for this priest. As it turned out, the previous priest was neither performing the ceremony nor attending on that day, and the priest who was officiating was absolutely delightful. He kept advising us all to go with the flow, not to worry if the kids were noisy, and to remember that we were in God's house, which is a place to rejoice. He was so laid back and pleasant. The lesson? Couples, choose your officiant well because it really makes a difference.

It also helps to have an officiant who is comfortable with a wedding planner's presence and participation. I once suggested to a pastor that we have a lit votive candle hidden behind the unity candle so that the mothers wouldn't have to fuss with actual matches during the ceremony, and he welcomed this suggestion. But I have also encountered many officiants who want nothing to do with me at all. When I called one priest on behalf of a couple from out of town who thought they might want to be married at his church, he bristled and said that he wouldn't talk to a wedding consultant—only to the bride and groom. Believe it or not, I have been told this a number of times.

In my experience, the best officiants are those who bring people together. At one wedding with a Jewish bride and a Muslim groom, the officiant (a friend of the family who happened to be Catholic) spoke about the goodness and love of peace that both faiths share, and I once witnessed a rabbi asking to have his photo taken with the priest with whom he was co-officiating so he could put it on his website. His card said, "Specializing in Wedding Ceremonies from Canada to the Caribbean … Interfaith, Jewish Traditional, Non-denominational and Civil. Commitment Ceremonies. French-Spanish-Italian-German." He proudly told me later that he had written the ceremony himself in both French and English. Now that's inclusive!

Even a nonreligious officiant can bring something to a ceremony that is unique and lovely and makes all the participants feel connected; one officiant I worked with at a mixed marriage (Jewish bride, Christian groom) created a flower circle by asking the groom's aunts to scatter petals around the couple while they were under the chuppah. Then he said, "I invite you, bride and groom, and all here present to view this circle as an intimate space where you will exchange your marriage vows. Thus, even as you are surrounded by the loving presence of family and friends, here in this circle, you are uniquely together."

So I offer all my clients the same advice about choosing an officiant as I do about choosing any other wedding professional: remember that this person will be with you for your wedding day. Follow your gut, and ask yourself these simple questions:

Do I like this person?

Does his/her approach feel right to me and for us?

Weddings are full of high stakes and high emotions, and you want your officiant to be the rock that keeps you grounded—the person who, when you get to the front of the aisle and find yourself standing there in front of your family and friends, smiles and without saying a word lets you know that you've come to the right place, that this moment is just as it was meant to be, and that all is well with the world.

At one wedding, the groom's uncle, who was not a member of the clergy, was asked to officiate the wedding ceremony. The uncle and I both arrived early at the rehearsal, and I asked him if he wanted to run it. He said absolutely not, and he didn't ask me any questions. When the bridal party was assembled, I lined them all up in the places where they were going to stand and then said to the uncle that the ceremony was all his. He looked at me and the couple and announced that while he had written some words about the bride and groom, he had no clue how to do the vows or rings! How could this be? He'd had many months to draft a ceremony, which was what I had been told he was doing.

Everyone stood there stunned, so I told him that I would go home and draft a ceremony for him. Fortunately, I have quite an assortment of ceremonies from prior weddings, so I "borrowed" parts and tried to insert them where they belonged—including a general greeting, readings by two of the guests, the uncle's words about the couple, the vows and exchange of rings, a blessing, the pronouncement as husband and wife, and finally the all-important kiss—using the program that the couple had already printed for their guests as a guide. I then e-mailed it to the uncle at eleven o'clock. Cobbling a ceremony together was not in my plans for Friday night, but we all know that plans can change, right? Grr.

The guests were already seated in the dining room, and we looked all over for the reverend who was supposed to give the blessing before the meal. We couldn't find him anywhere, and we wasted about twenty minutes looking for him before we decided to find a substitute. He never showed up. The next day, I sent him an e-mail:

> *Just wanted to let you know that the bride and groom had anticipated that you would give the blessing at the reception, and they were looking for you to do so.*

His reply?

> *Oh dear, I completely forgot!*

It was not a Jewish ceremony, and the bride and groom had never mentioned to me that they were going to break a glass. We had not discussed it at the rehearsal, and it never appeared on the timeline. So the officiant improvised, using one of the wine glasses from the hotel that was not wrapped in anything. Fortunately, the glass didn't go flying all over. Note to couples: before you decide to break something, talk to us first!

For one rehearsal, I arrived at the church early and found the doors locked. I called the parish office at 5:37 p.m., and the priest answered. I told him that I was there for a wedding rehearsal, to which he responded that the rehearsal would start at six. I said yes, that was the right time, but I asked if I could come in earlier because it was twenty degrees outside, and I was standing in the cold. He said the doors would open at 5:50 p.m., and he wouldn't open them sooner.

When the doors finally opened, I went up to the priest, introduced myself, and told him that I was the wedding coordinator. He replied, "Just so you know, you don't have anything to do with what happens in this church," in such a rude way. I have met many lovely members of the clergy, but he was not one of them.

One of the buses transporting guests to the ceremony left the hotel a little late, so I went up to the priest to tell him that the bus was on its way. He responded that the ceremony would start on time, regardless of whether the guests were there. I carefully mentioned this to the bridesmaids and asked them to take their time walking up the side stairs at the back of the church. Fortunately, they delayed long enough that the bus arrived and guests were walking in just when the priest wanted the bridal party to start processing, so he was forced to wait until the guests had entered and been seated.

The week before the wedding, we found out that there was *no* air-conditioning in the church, but they did have palm fans—some of which were advertisements for a *funeral* home and others of which had religious images. The bride hadn't realized that there was no air-conditioning; I assume that the church told her in the course of the planning, but she just didn't focus on it at the time. So the guests had to use the fans that were available. Note: if you are getting married in an old historic church in summer, remember to check to see if there is air-conditioning.

One pastor asked me at the rehearsal if there was going to be an aisle runner, and I said no. Then, right before the ceremony, he told me that a *paper* one had been delivered. I made an executive decision not to use it—the aisle was very narrow, and there was a heating grate in it. If the grate were covered, a woman's heel would surely go right through the runner. Too dangerous!

One bride asked me:

> *Can you or your assistant keep random gawkers out of the church? I ask because I've seen so many wedding photos that have people standing in the back of the church in jeans and T-shirts, and it just ruins the exit photos. I understand that people like to watch weddings, but I don't want to walk into the church and have the first and last people I see be strangers. Is this a totally ridiculous request?*

I replied:

> *Since it is clearly a public place, all we can and will do is ask any extra visitors to stay*

*seated. But in my experience at this particular
church, gawkers haven't been a problem at all.*

And they weren't.

I once worked with an especially terrific reverend who
was casually dressed and had a manner to match. He
had a couple of great lines at the rehearsal: "There will
be no bride's side or groom's side, because that turns
into the Hatfields and the McCoys." And "We are all in
agreement that what goes on tomorrow is exactly what
we had planned today. No one but those here will know
the difference!" And "Don't worry about your part.
Everyone will just be looking at the dress!" He couldn't
have been nicer, and he really put everyone at ease.

The ceremony went beautifully, and at the reception,
he stood up to give the blessing and said, "Thank God it
isn't as hot in here as it was in the church. And no, that
is not my toast." Toward the end of the night, he came
over to me, shook my hand, complimented me on my
work, and asked me to send him some of my business
cards, which I gladly did because he was so stellar and
personally contributed to make it a truly festive, joyous
occasion.

One wedding was at a distinguished local church, but
the bride's priest from her hometown parish was to
officiate. He came up to me at the rehearsal and said

that the place was "inhospitable" and that he would never perform another wedding there.

I was surprised, but toward the end of the rehearsal, I saw what he meant. I told the deacon that I had not worked there before and requested that he show me where the musicians would be sitting so I could cue them. He replied that the musicians would know when to start and that they would start on time, and that "if the bride is ready, she will get married, and if she isn't, she won't." Wow.

The next time I was at that church, I knew what to expect. Still, I was hopeful. I walked in and reintroduced myself to the deacon who was running the rehearsal, and I gave him my name and said, "I'm the wedding coordinator."

He responded, "Well, good for you." Such attitude.

I arrived at one church rehearsal to find a very authoritative "church lady" taking charge. I became invisible, and she totally ran the show. I had been warned, however, because the parish wedding guidelines had specifically said (in writing), "Wedding Coordinators are not encouraged. The Bride and Groom, as the ministers of this sacrament, are the only valid coordinators of their wedding."

The rabbi was due at five o'clock, with the ketubah signing scheduled for 5:30 p.m. At about 5:25 p.m., the rabbi wasn't there, so I called him on his cell, and a woman answered. I introduced myself and then asked when the rabbi would be there. She answered that he would be there soon and hung up. He didn't arrive until about a quarter to six. He said to me, "I apologize for being late, but you don't have a wife."

One bride and groom asked me if they could have some private time right after the ceremony, before cocktail hour. A guest gave me a Private for the Bride and Groom sign, which I put on the door right after they went inside. As I was doing this, the rabbi came upstairs. I told him that the couple was in the room, but he said he was going in to take off his robe. He knocked on the door and said something like, "I hope you're not doing anything in there."

One bride-to-be was going through the conversion process to become Catholic. The wedding was to be held in a historic church, and the groom's family had been given special dispensation to have the wedding held there even though the conversion process would not be completed by the wedding date.

A few weeks before the wedding, the mother of the bride showed her daughter's future mother-in-law the programs that she had printed. The groom's mother freaked out when she saw them because Communion wasn't listed as part of the ceremony.

The bride and groom had planned the ceremony themselves and had omitted Communion in order to be sensitive to the bride's family, but the mother of the groom wouldn't let it go, so suddenly Communion was on the agenda, and the programs were being reprinted. I was told by the bride's mother that the groom's family had "obviously paid *someone* so that Communion could be part of the Mass!" She said that she felt like a steamroller has gone right over her. And then she wondered aloud, "How much does it cost to get into heaven?"

One priest's admonition to the men at the rehearsal: "Don't tailgate in the church's parking lot before the wedding!"

A certain very good-looking young priest performed two weddings in which I have been involved. One of the brides told me off the record that he is known as Father What-a-Waste—because he is so hot!

The reverend was invited to the wedding reception and dinner, where he was supposed to give a blessing. He picked up his place card at cocktail hour and told me that he didn't want to stay for dinner. He said that he felt bad because his meal was already paid for, but that judging by what he saw of the event, it "wouldn't make a dent." *Oh my.*

One rabbi was very difficult to work with. I sent him a copy of the timeline a week before the wedding and requested that he send me a reply so I'd know that he received it, but I received no word from him. Then, on the day of the wedding, he was supposed to arrive at three o'clock, and the ketubah ceremony was slated for 3:30. He waltzed in with no apologies at 3:40 p.m. My assistant asked him about his preference for the order of the processional, but he told her he didn't care.

The ketubah ceremony didn't start until about four o'clock, which was when the ceremony had been scheduled. Then the rabbi wanted to have a *badeken* (the traditional Jewish veiling ceremony)—even though the bride and groom were not observant Jews—so that delayed things even further. Thus, we were behind schedule by about a half hour or more all night.

To top it all off, the groom's mother had provided a frame for the ketubah, but it didn't fit. My assistant and I had to tape it onto the fabric lining of the easel at the ceremony so all could see it. Not exactly perfect, but we made it work. I think that was the metaphor for the entire evening!

I got to the church early for the rehearsal, and the door was locked. I figured it was just locked because I had arrived too soon. When two of the bridal party appeared, I called the rectory and was told that someone would come and open the door. About ten minutes later (with most of the wedding party now standing outside in the hot sun), I called again, and the woman said that she had sent some guy over. About five or ten minutes later, I pestered her again, and the woman said that they couldn't find the keys before but had just now found them, and someone was coming over. I asked when we might expect that person to arrive, and she said in ten minutes! It was ninety-two degrees, the heat was absolutely sweltering, and everyone just stood in the shade and made do as best they could. Someone with the keys finally came a few minutes after the last call.

The rabbi was supposed to be at the venue for the ketubah signing at a quarter after six. I had spoken to him during the week and e-mailed the timeline, which he obviously ignored. He arrived at around seven o'clock instead, had the witnesses sign the ketubah, said about two sentences to the bride and groom, and that was that. It was shocking and disappointing—he barely went through the motions.

At the rehearsal, the altar flower arrangements were partially filled with white lilies left over from Easter, and the bride and her mother made a big deal about having them removed. First of all, they were droopy because Easter had been the previous week, and second of all, it wasn't the look they were going for, since their altar flowers and pew bouquets were going to be a soft, colorful mix. The priest was very reluctant, but he said okay.

The next day, an hour before the wedding, I received a call from the florist telling me that the church absolutely would not move the lilies out. The mother of the bride was beside herself. I dialed the church and handed her my phone, and she spoke directly to a priest—not the one from the rehearsal, who supposedly did not have the authority to move the flowers—but it did not go well. He accused her of being "in denial of the liturgical season" and made it clear, in no uncertain terms, that the Easter lilies would not be removed.

So we had to live with them, and the mother of the bride was distraught about it all day. It really wasn't that big a deal, but somehow it ruined the wedding for her.

At the end of the ceremony, the woman from the rectory office told me that the pink petals on the steps to the church would have to be removed before the next Mass. I looked at her with a dumbfounded expression. Then I asked for a broom. She provided a broom, dustpan, and small brush, and thus I took the box from the boutonnieres and filled it three or four times with rose petals and tossed them out. Later in the evening, I mentioned this to the florist, and she said that her guys were on their way to the church at that moment to do the pickup/cleanup. Too late!

One priest, a family friend, forgot his suit at the home of the parents of the bride. The mother of the bride had to enlist a friend, a key, and a car to get it brought to the church in time for the wedding.

Once I e-mailed a church to inquire about the guest parking. Their terse response: "It is the responsibility of the couple to consult with us regarding such questions. We deal directly with the couple in all matters pertaining to the wedding. This information was provided in writing to the couple when they scheduled their wedding date with us. Perhaps they can share that information with you."

From one bride to me:

> *Below you'll find the email and attachments that I sent to the Pastor. Hopefully he will realize that I am a bridezilla and that not showing up at the specified time could potentially be hazardous for him!* ☺

And the pastor's response to the bride:

> *My goodness, what organizational skills … lol! Don't worry, everything will be fine. Yes, I'll deliver the blessing at the reception. Also, I have yet to officiate at a wedding that starts on time. Don't let 'precision and exactness' worry*

you, instead think 'process and capturing the
moment.' This is once in a lifetime. Absorb the
sanctity of the occasion.

Always good advice!

One officiant enjoyed the reception, and late in the
evening, she came up to me to see if I had any deodorant
that she could borrow. She had been dancing up a
storm! I went to my kit and gave it to her, glad that she
was enjoying the party.

To a wedding planner, a rehearsal usually means
that you give everyone a quick verbal overview of the
ceremony and then line them up for a dry run. But not
this time.

The participants were told to arrive at 5:30, and
the rehearsal was supposed to start at a quarter to six.
Instead, it started at six o'clock, and the priest *talked*
through *the entire ceremony.* He described every single
prayer and every detail, so the rehearsal lasted for an
hour and twenty minutes. In my experience, that is a
record. At about 6:50 p.m., I suggested to the mother
of the bride that she call the restaurant where the
rehearsal dinner was to take place to tell them that
they would be late.

At the rehearsal, we had planned that the groom would walk down the aisle with his parents, followed by the bridal party in pairs, and then finally the bride with her parents. But on the wedding day, suddenly there was a grandmother walking with the groom's dad, another set of the groom's grandparents, two uncles, and the groom's aunt in the lineup. We hadn't reserved seats up front for any of them, because no one had told us they would be walking. So there was quite a lot of rushing around at the last minute.

The Russian Orthodox wedding ceremony requires that the bride and groom, bridal party, and *all* the guests remain standing for almost all of it. I went out in the hallway to sit on the steps for about fifteen or twenty minutes. It's hard to stand on marble, and I knew I would be on my feet all night. On the plus side, almost the entire service is sung a cappella. Beautiful.

The guest buses and the wedding party bus were right on time at two o'clock. The groom and his men went on the wedding party bus, and the guest bus departed right after. But when they arrived at the church for the three o'clock ceremony, there was another wedding going on. It turned out that the one o'clock ceremony hadn't started until 1:50 p.m. So we had to figure out what to do with the guests, since they couldn't go into the church, and there was something going on in the lower level of the church as well. But the bus *had* to drop the guests off and turn around to go back and pick up more guests at the hotel. *Ugh.*

Our ceremony finally started at 3:11 p.m., which was pretty good in light of how late the other ceremony ended. But the church lady was beyond horrible, pushing us to rush, rush, rush, pushing the musicians to start before everyone was in place, and trying to get the bridesmaids to walk in before the processional music had started.

Then the priest delivered a long homily, so the ceremony didn't end until about 4:20 p.m. or so. The biggest problem was that it was getting dark, and the bridal party photos and portraits of the bride and groom were still to come. The photographer did his best and took as many photos as possible with the available light and then took more photos in the venue. Fortunately, the light ended up looking rather atmospheric, and the couple ultimately had beautiful wedding images.

One couple had planned to have a close relative perform the ceremony, but even though he had been ordained online, they were concerned about the legality of the ceremony in the future. A few weeks before the wedding, the groom e-mailed me:

> *I spoke to my fiancée this weekend and she agrees that having a second officiant officially marry us just before the wedding ceremony is the way to go. If you could help us find such a person, that would be great. I almost don't care who it is, as long as they have the*

required status in a religious institution, as opposed to just an online ordainment. This second officiant will need to prepare pretty much nothing as far as a ceremony goes, hopefully wouldn't need to meet with us in advance (though I understand that might not be possible), and hopefully will therefore be relatively inexpensive.

I contacted a clergyman who agreed to come and sign the formal license on the day of the wedding at the venue where both the ceremony and reception were being held.

You have to love it when a priest closes his prayer before dinner with these words:

Bless our food
Bless our dancing
And bless our drinking!

6. *Mirror, Mirror on the Wall*

The Quest for Beauty and Perfection

*T*here is so much hype in the wedding industry—on television, in movies, in magazines, and online—about hair, makeup, and attire and the role they should play in your "perfect" day. In my experience, this focus on the more superficial aspects of the wedding day puts an enormous amount of pressure on the brides and their mothers, sisters, grandmothers, nieces, and aunts, bridesmaids, and even groomsmen too, and this is really unfortunate. No aspect of a wedding produces more tears than hair, makeup, and the choice of the all-important dress (for both the bride *and* her bridesmaids—I have seen more squabbles over bridesmaids' dresses than just about anything else). One bride was perfectly fine with having me choose her invitations and cake without consulting her but had me do *seven* hair-and-makeup timelines for six people having these processes done until we got the schedule "exactly right." Go figure.

It all comes back to that Barbie wedding dress. The truth is that many of us have been thinking about our wedding day and about how we will look as a bride since we were very young. It's our day to feel beautiful, to be glamorous, to be the star of the show. We get to swap our jeans and work attire for an actual ball gown and have a team of professionals fuss over us and make us look every bit as fabulous as any celebrity or supermodel. I had one bride who had purchased her wedding shoes years before she even met her groom; she saw them in a store when she was nineteen and decided then and there that she would wear them at her future wedding. The pressure to look perfect—to be thin enough, tan enough, to have the perfect updo or the perfect French manicure—is huge, and it can bring out the worst in almost anyone.

Even other family members and friends are not immune to the pressures of perfection that surround a wedding. I had one bride who didn't typically wear makeup, but the mother of the groom wanted her to wear it for the engagement photo shoot. I explained to the future mother-in-law that these were very informal shots and that the photographer would create a sign-in book from these images that would be used at the wedding and then belong to the bride and groom. Since these weren't the official wedding photos, I suggested that she pick her battles, but she didn't listen to my advice and kept pushing the matter, and long story short, the bride wore makeup for the photos. Similarly, I had another bride who wanted to wear a tiara, but her future mother-in-law said, "Only a beauty pageant winner, the Queen of England, or Grace Kelly should wear a tiara." In this case also, the bride didn't get her way.

Because beauty and the process of getting ready are a key part of any "successful" wedding, I always arrive on the day of the event with an emergency kit packed with items to solve any wardrobe crisis and help everyone look their best. My favorite request came from one bridesmaid who asked me if I had an extra thong! And believe it or not, I have since had the same request at other weddings. So even though I didn't have a thong for the first bridesmaid who asked, I definitely had one for the second. (Turns out there is a company that makes thongs in very small tins, which are perfect for my purposes.) I once came back into the bridal suite to find that my emergency kit had been opened and ransacked—in the whirlwind of getting ready, the bridesmaids had gone into it by themselves and torn the whole thing apart, which was a first. I could tell that stress levels were running high, so I urged the women to eat some of the food that had been provided by room service. Everyone felt better and calmer after they had a bite to eat—and a sip of champagne.

The biggest help to a bride in these matters is almost always her support team, and that goes for the groom too. When everyone around you is telling you that you look gorgeous/handsome/stunning/amazing/wonderful, it is hard to disregard it. The "stars" of the show feel best about themselves when they have their posse on hand encouraging them, and as a wedding planner, it's my job to find practical ways to mitigate any beauty-related stress. Who can tie the sash properly? Your wedding planner can! Who can bustle your gown? I have done *so* many different bustles and promise that I can definitely do yours. Who can tie a bow tie? I can do it, but I have an assistant who is absolutely *great* at it. The important thing to remember is that at the end of the day, a wedding is not about the loose strand of hair or the slightly irregular pocket square or the bridesmaid who refused to wear silver sandals. It's about the connection and deep commitment that exists between the couple, their families, and their friends. Period.

Before the couple heads down the aisle, I always remind them to stop for a second and look at the people who are assembled there. These are *their people*. When else do we get to have all the people we love most and who love us back gathered together in one place? The love that surrounds a wedding and the shared joy of those who come to witness it is what makes the event and all the participants beautiful—not a dress.

We were at a resort south of the border for a wedding, and I was there as the assistant to another wedding consultant. We received a phone call from the bride at 6:22 a.m. on the *morning* of the wedding. She was hysterical because she couldn't open her eye. The consultant went to her room immediately, and I went down to the front desk to locate a doctor.

The doctor arrived and discovered that there was a mascara bristle stuck in the bride's eye. The doctor removed it and gave her an oral antibiotic as well as anti-inflammatory eyedrops. The bride was told to use both and to not wear any eye makeup for several days. Even so, the bride wore eye makeup *and* false eyelashes for her wedding later that day.

At one wedding, the bride's gown was fitted so closely that there was no room underneath for a push-up bra. She and her friend found a unique solution to this, and I stood by for moral support as the friend used *duct tape* to tape her breasts together so that they wouldn't go below the stays in the gown. As the photographer quipped, "It's like they were stuffing ten pounds of s—— into a four-pound bag." The tape worked, but we were all just waiting for something to spill out of the *top* of the bride's gown! And I shudder to think about how she got undressed at the end of the night.

Almost all the bridesmaids' dresses needed steaming, so I was busy all morning with my trusty steamer.

Then I packed up the steamer, and my assistant took it downstairs to the hotel's concierge desk so we could pick it up quickly as we left.

After dressing, the bride and bridesmaids were supposed to meet back in the same room where they had had their hair and makeup done, and then we would all to proceed to the trolley. I distributed the flowers to the women, and we were almost out the door when the bride decided to present her attendants with gifts (earrings and necklaces). The trolley was downstairs waiting, and here they were, opening gifts. Grr. And then, one of the bridesmaids walked in, all dressed, and announced that she had decided that that *her* dress needed steaming. But the steamer was already in the concierge's closet downstairs, and it was past time to go. I had to tell her to let the photographer Photoshop out the wrinkles.

One bride's dress was about two inches too long, and I blew through all my safety pins pinning it up! But it worked, and the pins only showed very slightly. Did anyone think of trying it on ahead of time?

One bride was getting ready for the ceremony when someone handed her a wrapped box. As she opened it, she told us that she already knew what it was: a gift from the groom, a pair of earrings that she had seen at the store when they were shopping for his cufflinks. She also said that she had loved the earrings and wanted them for the wedding, but the groom "couldn't afford them." She said this right in front of me and all the bridesmaids and the groom's mother too.

The bride had a detachable train. I helped remove it, and then I bustled the gown—*three* times. The first was the regular bustle. During the night, someone stepped on her gown, and I had to pin the bustle back up with three pins. Later, they were ripped out too, and I had to pin the gown again just as I was leaving.

I had one very demanding bride who sent me a snippy e-mail:

> *I know you couldn't come to today's dress fitting because it's a Saturday* [Yes, it was a Saturday, and I had a *wedding!*] *but the date for me to pick up the dress is Wednesday, July 11th, at 11 am. My mother and I ask that you join us since my bridesmaids are unable to make it and we'd like someone in addition to my mother to know how to bustle my specific dress. We specifically chose a weekday morning so that you won't have a wedding conflict, and the wedding is six weeks away and we haven't had you attend anything with us other than the catering meeting. Please let me know if you can make it.*

I responded as politely as I could:

> *I have attached a copy of your contract and also our Services and Pricing information. As you can see, the Experience that you have chosen does not include any vendor visits on my part. However, I will extend a courtesy to you and attend your fitting, even though this is beyond the scope of our agreement.*
>
> *I can understand your concern about your bustle, but please rest assured that I have done a zillion different bustles! In fact, there never seem to be two that are the same.*
>
> *While there are variations, there are typically three or four main kinds, and I have always been able to do them. So, please relax … and know that I will join you on the 11ᵗʰ.*

Thankfully, the bride and her mother were appreciative that I went with them to the fitting.

On her wedding day, one bride sat in the salon in tears because she hated the way her hair had been styled. There was a lot of confusion in the salon because all the women wanted their hair done, but the stylist had only planned to do the bride's hair and her mother's. So she had to rush, and apparently this led to a less-than-perfect hairstyle for the bride. When the bride returned to her suite, she was still upset, so a bridesmaid ordered a bottle of wine from room service to help her calm down. And later I was told that no one tipped anyone in the salon, so I am sure there were hard feelings all the way around.

For one wedding, I suggested that we have a shoe check instead of a coat check at the venue. The hotel wasn't far from the venue, so there was the expectation that guests would walk. But women walking six long blocks while wearing high heels on a hot summer day was not ideal, so I suggested that the bridal party and the female guests wear flats to the venue, carry their party shoes, and change before the wedding began.

Men: try on your tuxedos (especially if you are renting them)—and check all the buttons, zippers, and any other moving parts before the wedding day! One groom popped his jacket button as he knelt during the ceremony, so I had to take the boutonniere pin that I always store inside my jacket lapel and use it to close his jacket for photos. At another wedding, we noticed while waiting to begin the processional that the father of the bride's pants were hemmed *way* too long. My assistant grabbed a needle and thread and shortened them on the spot.

I had never seen a bride and groom give their guests specific directions about attire for a wedding—but on their website, the bride and groom included this:

1920s Garden Party
Come ready to rock the garden party Gatsby-style!
We mean it! Hats, pearls, feathers,
flapper dresses, smart tweeds
Required viewing includes Baz Luhrmann's
Gatsby, coming out May 10
and check out the new Gatsby
Brooks Brothers collection

A few guests got into the spirit, but most did not—although the bride and groom were suitably attired. She wore in a Gatsby-inspired gown, and he was in a khaki suit.

One bride's dress did *not* zip up. We called the bridal salon, and they were going to send someone out. We had enough time for that, but emotions were running high. The mother of the bride and a friend of hers were both seamstress types, and first the mother of the bride tried soap on the zipper, but it didn't work. Then I gave them a big safety pin to place in the end of the zipper, and they were finally able to yank it up. Luckily, I was able to cancel the visit by the salon's seamstress before she left her shop.

I had one bridesmaid who didn't fill out the top of her dress properly, so I stuffed it with tulle and affixed double-sided tape between the dress and her chest to hold everything together.

At one wedding, the bride and bridesmaids were having their hair done at the couple's home. Several of the women were unhappy with the results, and the bride had her hair done, hated it, had it done again … and yet again. After the hair stylist left, she pulled her hair out of the updo totally and put in hot rollers. I am not sure why she didn't continue to speak up, but she was upset and finally just took matters into her own hands. She knew the hair stylist well and had done a trial before the wedding, but there was a lot of family drama surrounding the actual day, and I think that ultimately, the only thing she could control was her hair. She was not a happy bride.

On the morning of the wedding, at the home of the bride's father, the photographer was taking photos of the bride's gown and asked for the veil. The father called the bride, who was still at the hair salon, and it turns out she had forgotten to pick it up at the wedding boutique. Fortunately, one of the father's friends, who lived near the shop, picked it up and brought it to the bride.

One groomsman had forgotten his bow tie. No problem, I thought, as I had one in my emergency kit, right in my car, which was sitting right in front of the hotel as I had requested. I got the tie and then went back up to see the men, only to discover that they were wearing champagne-colored ties, and mine was black. So I gave the black one to the ring bearer, and his champagne-colored one was worn by the groomsman. No one would ever notice.

I was with one bride and her mother when the bride tried to get into her gown. The gown would *not* close. The bride was tiny, and I don't know how this happened, but obviously she hadn't tried on the gown after the last fitting. She had bra cups basted into the dress, and I had to cut them out. Still, the dress was too tight with the hook and eye closed, so I suggested that she just leave it unhooked. It was okay then, but what a cautionary tale!

I had brought my whole emergency kit to the hotel, as usual, so I would have everything handy when the women were getting ready, and I did not use *one* item from my emergency kit the whole night! This was an absolute first.

When I was at the salon with the bridal party overseeing hair and makeup, the bride told me that one of the bridesmaids' dresses didn't fit right, and could I please see if I could zip it up? Sure. But when I saw it, I thought, *Are you kidding me?* The dress didn't fit by a *mile;* there were probably five or six inches separating the two sides of the zipper! I suggested that she go upstairs, where there was fortunately a dress shop, and see if they could do something for her. She ended up pinning the two sides together and purchasing a white silk shawl to cover the back of her dress.

After the ceremony, my assistant and I walked back to the reception venue. We sat in the getting-ready suite, and the photographer called to say that the groom's ivory vest had lost *all six* of its buttons, and he couldn't continue taking photos. My assistant went to a tuxedo store a few blocks away to get new buttons (with the idea that I was going to sew them on) because when I called the original store, their only suggestion was to have the groom go to their location in another town and get a new vest. Of course there was no time to do that, but the downtown store, which was right near where we were, didn't have one. The immediate issue was timing and photos, so instead of getting new buttons for me to sew, the groom dropped his ivory vest off at the store and picked up a black one, which he wore for the photos while the store sewed the buttons back on the ivory one for him. When the store was finished, my assistant picked up the ivory vest so the groom would have it for the reception, and later she returned the borrowed black one back to the shop.

One bride and groom and their bridal party went around the town to take photos before the wedding. The bride's stiletto heels were absolutely brown when she came back, so I took chalk and made them white once more.

The bride's aunt had bought new shoes for the wedding, but she bought them a size too big because they were the only size left in the store and were such a bargain. She was slipping out of the shoes as she walked, though, and came to see if I could help. Moleskin to the rescue.

At one wedding, I helped the bride get into her gown. Her dress had a pretty row of buttons up the back, and I had just assumed they were on a zipper. *Wrong.* Every single one needed buttoning. I had a crochet hook but thought it might be faster if I buttoned by hand. Suddenly, something sharp pierced my finger. The buttons were actually made of pieces of metal covered in fabric, and a drop of blood ended up on the button. Fortunately, a Tide to Go stick worked perfectly to remove it—a real commercial for the product.

I went to bustle the bride's gown, and one of the strings came right off in my hand. As always, I had my carryall with a sewing kit inside, and I had to sew the string back on before I could continue with the bustle. I managed to thread the needle, but I think I was just lucky. Note to self: have a needle threader handy at all times!

The father of the bride forgot his tuxedo shirt and only had a plain white shirt. He was wearing a vest, and I don't think anyone would have noticed, but the bride was very upset and angry. I made a quick call to a men's store a few blocks away, and when I heard that they had an appropriate shirt in the father's size, I requested that they bring the shirt (steamed and on a hanger) to the hotel within the next fifteen minutes. (I put it on my credit card and was reimbursed by the dad.) Amazingly, the store delivered the shirt, but they arrived a few minutes late, so I sent the bride and her parents to the church in the car that had been ordered, and as soon as the shirt arrived, I jumped into a taxi. I actually got to the church before the bride and her parents, and the dad had time to quickly change.

I bustled one bride's gown that had *twenty sets* of strings! That was, in my experience, a record.

7. *The Best Laid Plans* ...

Mishaps and Mayhem

*T*here are always things you don't count on with any wedding. At one wedding, we all got drenched from rain, and the following weekend, everyone was wilting in ninety-seven-degree heat. There will almost certainly be things that go wrong, mishaps, and mistakes, but most can be corrected, either with creativity, scissors, a glue gun, or a smile. I bring along my huge emergency kit and am prepared for most minor glitches. And as with any unwelcome surprise, a sense of humor goes a long way.

At one wedding, all the preparations went like clockwork. Makeup at the home of the bride's parents was finished. The photographer was there, the bride looked beautiful in her dress, the flowers were gorgeous, and the Rolls-Royce specially ordered for the bride and her parents—along with the minibus for the bridal party—all arrived as planned. We all got to the church with plenty of time and saw that the rest of the wedding party had assembled. But then when the mother of the bride got out of the Rolls, she tipped her "tussy-mussy"—the holder for her small bouquet—and water spilled all down the front of her dress. Fortunately, she was terrific and took it in stride. She saw some people sitting on a balcony of the apartment building next to the church and simply called up to them and asked to borrow a hair dryer. My assistant went with her and dried the dress, and amazingly, they were still on time for the ceremony. In this case, quick thinking and a little luck saved the day.

These are my main strategies for avoiding mishaps: 1) Repeatedly ask myself and others, "What if?" throughout the planning process. What if it rains? What if it's too hot? What if lunch isn't delivered on time? What if the readers don't have their readings? What if the officiant forgets to bring the ceremony wording itself? (As I am sure you can imagine by now, I have answers for all of these.) 2) Check and double-check everything. At virtually every wedding, my assistants and I go around the reception room with the guest list and seating chart in hand and literally count the table settings (yes, the plates, napkins, glasses, and silverware) and the chairs. We make sure that the centerpieces, table numbers, and anything else that is supposed to be there has appeared and been set up as planned. 3) Carry an extensive emergency kit—mine is actually a suitcase—that contains all kinds of items, including:

◊ Advil (Even though I make it a practice to never hand out or dispense medications—I simply put the bottle on the table, and someone can pick it up if he or she feels the need to.)

◊ Alcohol (Not the drinking kind. Once I had to swab a bridesmaid's ear that was bleeding.)

◊ Baby aspirin (If someone is having a heart attack, this might be important before professional help arrives!)

◊ Baby powder (for putting in shoes to absorb perspiration and reduce friction)

◊ Bandages, including spray-on bandages and special bandages for blisters

◊ Batteries (for candlesticks in venues that don't permit live flames)

◊ Blotting paper

◊ Bobby pins (for securing the flower girl's crown, bride's veil, men's yarmulkes)

◊ Bottle opener, corkscrew

◊ Cake knife (in case the venue doesn't have a proper cake knife—which happens)

◊ Chalk (which can be used to cover up spots on bride's gown, flower girl's dress, bride's or flower girl's shoes)

◊ Cold packs, the kind that don't drip (To be used in hot weather. I keep these on the bus for the bridal party when it is hot outside.)

◊ Cough drops

◊ Crochet hook (for hooking the buttons on the wedding gown)

◊ Dental floss

◊ Deodorant

◊ Earplugs (for wedding professionals, guests, and me when the music is way too loud)

◊ Envelopes (empty ones for hosts who want to give a gratuity)

◊ Extra escort cards and reserved seat cards (for dinner or the ceremony)

◊ Evian spray (for the bride/bridal party on a hot day while taking photos outside)

◊ Fans (hand-held and battery-operated)

◊ Flashlight (especially for outdoor weddings)

◊ Floral pins (to secure buttons and boutonnieres)

◊ Gas-X

◊ Glue gun (You'd be amazed at what can be fixed or secured with a glue gun; a planner can't leave home without it!)

◊ Guest lists (alphabetically and by table number to assist guests in finding their seats and to determine where a guest is sitting if an escort card has inadvertently been omitted)

◊ Hair dryer (to dry spills and, of course, for hair)

◊ Hair spray

◊ Hand cream

◊ Hanger with mesh covering (Believe it or not, that funny little piece of spongy material that covers the hanger can be rubbed on clothing to remove deodorant stains. It works brilliantly!)

◊ Imodium

◊ Lightbulb (for the groom to step on in Jewish ceremony instead of a glass, as it is easier to break)

◊ Lighter (with long handle for lighting candles on dinner tables)

◊ Lint remover

◊ Makeup sponge (for blotting and removing deodorant stains—works like the hanger cover)

◊ Marker, black

◊ Matches (To light a votive candle at ceremony. I like to light it and hide it behind a unity candle and then have participants use the votive to light their candles rather than try to fiddle with lighted matches. Also, sometimes I light candles at the reception and blow them out immediately, as it is easier to light a candle that has been lit before.)

◊ Mints and Listerine strips

◊ Moleskin (for shoes and for protecting skin from sharp objects, like a piece of metal on a wrist corsage)

◊ Money (supply change; for taxis, incidentals for which I will be reimbursed)

◊ Nail clipper

◊ Nail file

◊ Nail polish (clear, to touch up fingers and toes and repair stocking/pantyhose runs)

◊ Neosporin

◊ Parasols for sun (Usually I bring a half dozen.)

◊ Pashminas (I bring enough for the bridal party.)

◊ Pepto-Bismol

◊ Pens (For ketubah, calligraphy, sign-in. One pen should be a permanent marker but not one that will bleed through the special papers.)

◊ Petals (For the cake table. I have artificial petals if we need them for photos but of course prefer real ones.)

◊ Photo list (of who is in photos and what shots the photographer needs to get)

◊ Pins and safety pins (lots of them—to hold up hems or the bustle of the bride's gown or lots of other uses)

◊ Ponytail holders

◊ Power bars for the bride and groom (Often useful right before ceremony—especially if the bride has just had a gin and tonic!)

◊ Readings for ceremony, in *large* font

◊ Q-tips

◊ Ribbon (Either in the "wedding colors" or something neutral. Sometimes ribbon is draped over reserved seats for the ceremony to indicate that they are not open.)

◊ Rings (fake ones to put on the ring pillow for the procession)

◊ Sandpaper (for scuffing the soles of shoes so the wearer doesn't slip)

◊ Scissors (several pairs)

◊ Seam ripper (to remove itchy tags or labels)

◊ Sewing kit (My eleventh-hour quickie sewing jobs have included a father of the bride's pants that were too long, a father of the bride's pants that were too wide, a father of the groom's jacket button, a best man's jacket button, a groom's jacket button, a groom's vest, a bride's necklace, a flower girl's hem, and a bride's bustle strings—and I also bring *a needle threader*, as it's hard to do this kind of sewing under pressure and/or in dim light.)

◊ Shoe gels

◊ Shout Wipes, Tide to Go Instant Stain Remover, and other stain-removal aids (I have cleaned makeup stains, lotion stains, pigeon poop, horse poop, and more off many wedding gowns, bridesmaids' dresses, and tuxedo shirts and pants.)

◊ Solemates (clear plastic tips with wide bases for the heels of women's shoes so they can walk better in grass)

◊ Static cling spray

◊ Steamer (To take the wrinkles out of bridesmaids' sashes, bride's sashes, bride's gown, train and veil, bridesmaids' dresses, and pashminas, as well as men's ties, pocket squares, and shirts. I steam *something* at almost every wedding.)

◊ Straws (so the bride and bridesmaids can drink without destroying their lipstick)

◊ Tape:

    o Scotch (To hold things together. I even taped one mother of the bride's necklace to keep it fastened.)

    o Double-sided (to hold up hems, hide and secure bra straps, to quickly shorten groomsman's pants hem, to fix a bridesmaid's neckline, to remove lint)

    o Duct tape (clear, to hold down extension cords and runners, to secure rings inside a pocketbook, and, in one case mentioned in the previous chapter, the *bride's breasts*)

    o Fashion tape (for the bride's gown and many other odd uses)

    o Flower tape (to secure flowers and also candles)

    o CAUTION tape (to help close a road)

◊ Thongs (as discussed above)

◊ Ties (men's bow ties—as well as men's socks, suspenders, collar stays, cufflinks, studs, and tuxedo buttons)

◊ Tissues (I leave packets on the parents' pews/ seats at wedding, and one in the bride's bouquet—weddings can get very emotional!)

◊ Toothbrush and toothpaste

◊ Towels (to help the makeup artists or dry the bottoms of bouquets when they first come out of water)

◊ Trash bag (very large size for the bride to place under her gown during photos on a wet lawn; if necessary, I can also cut holes for legs and the bride can step in, pull the bag up, and walk in very wet weather while protecting her dress)

◊ Tulle (to fill out the bust line of the bridesmaid's dresses)

◊ Tylenol

◊ Umbrellas

◊ Visine

◊ Water (bottles for the bride and groom, musicians and other wedding professionals, including my team)

◊ Winter gloves (in case the bride may need them for an outdoor winter photo shoot)

On the day of the wedding, I scribble notes on the working timeline so that I know which items were used and which ones I need to repurchase or replenish before the next wedding. Scissors, hairspray, safety pins, fashion (and other kinds of) tape, and a glue gun are the most commonly used items. At one wedding, I had to laugh when the mother of the bride saw my suitcase and asked if she got to keep the kit. Yes, it looks impressive—but the answer would be *no*.

Preparedness, quick thinking, and a little ingenuity can go a long way to solving most wedding mishaps, and after ten years of practice, I like to think that I do a pretty good job. I have been hailed as the "savior of the wedding" by one bride and as a fairy godmother by another. But it's not magic that does the fixing, just the skills that come with experience and my genuine desire to make each wedding as perfect as it can possibly be. You can rest assured that most weddings turn out fabulously despite the inevitable bumps in the road— or, as they say, all's well that ends well. It seems that all that effort and planning pays off. Imagine that.

Shortly after I arrived at the church for the ceremony, a flower girl was holding her (heavy) basket overflowing with big red roses, and the bottom of the basket fell out, leaving her just holding a handle. I sat on the marble floor at the back of the church, plugged in my glue gun, and glued the handle back on. Not my most dignified moment, but at least the little girl had her basket.

The only time we could get together for a finalization meeting, based on the bride and groom's schedule, was on a Friday at 5:30 in the evening, so the bride, groom, banquet manager, and I scheduled a meeting then. The groom arrived a half hour late, and the bride was a no-show; she had decided to have her hair done without telling any of us ahead of time. The groom had no information, and the bride had it all, so we went into the wedding without having finalized any of the details.

Once in the middle of a reception, I spotted the groom sitting on a chair near the bathroom. I assumed that he was just waiting his turn, but after he'd been there awhile, I checked, and he said that he was waiting for the bride, who was in the getting-ready room across the hall. I walked in, and the bride was standing there in shorts and a button-down shirt, her gown thrown over a chair, looking miserable. She said that she was feeling sick and that she hadn't eaten a thing since breakfast.

I asked the groom to get the bride a glass of ginger ale and suggested that she sit down in the big chair and relax. I also suggested that what she probably needed more than anything was a good cry. She had been so emotional all day long leading up to the wedding, and she had already had one bout of tears over her hairdo. It looked to me like she was just holding in so many feelings. That was like giving her permission, and the floodgates suddenly opened up. The groom returned with the ginger ale and comforted her.

I stepped out of the room to tell the caterer that we wouldn't be doing any cake cutting just yet. Her new mother-in-law came in and must have said something helpful, because the next thing I knew, the bride had put her gown back on, she and the groom were ready to cut the cake, and the evening proceeded.

I told the maid of honor and best man that they would be alerted when it was time for their speeches, but the groomsmen were kind of on their own schedule, and the best man was pretty nervous. When the father of the bride sat down after his toast, we gave the kitchen the okay to serve the salads … but suddenly the best man was at the microphone. His nerves got the better of him, and he had jumped in to get it over with without even waiting for his cue.

I had one mother of the bride who started walking down the aisle with gum in her mouth. I quickly stepped in front of her, held out my hand, and she spit it out.

She was actually someone I had known for a long time, and she wrote me an e-mail after the wedding that said:

> *I promise to never walk down an aisle again with gum in my mouth. Well, I hope there won't be any more weddings on my side of the family anyway!*

At one wedding, the photographer first took photos at the church, and then she went with the entire family and bridal party into the city to do more photos at a location near the reception venue. When the photos were over, everyone went to get back on the waiting bus, but the bus wouldn't start. The bride, groom, and bridal party all ended up taking taxis to the venue.

The party decorator, whom the couple had hired without my input, had flats of wheatgrass in which she had inserted sticks of white chocolate lollipops. There was a small square pasted on each with the guests' names and table assignments, but the cursive writing was too small and hard to read. Furthermore, the grass flats were wet, and the lollipops had been inserted in the afternoon, so by the time the reception rolled around, their sticks had become soggy and started falling over. Some ideas that initially sound great just don't work. The decorator asked if she could "borrow" my assistants to help the guests obtain and decipher their lollipops, and that's what happened.

The wedding professionals were all sitting together eating dinner in a room adjacent to the ballroom when the photographer went out to check on the party. He came back and told me that I should know that an elderly man had collapsed at his table at dinner. I immediately went to the rotunda and checked with the banquet manager. Security handled the whole thing, but it took a while for the paramedics to arrive and take the man out. To this day, I have no idea what was wrong.

The day before the wedding, the groom told me that they had packed the car the night before and a thief had broken in and stolen all the wedding jewelry. Fortunately, it was all insured. Rule #1: Don't ever let those rings get out of your sight!

The flower girls walked down the aisle two by two. The first two were fine. One of the second pair dropped petals and then stopped and bent down to pick them back up, but her little partner didn't know what to do when she stopped, and she got hysterical. Her mother had to go and retrieve her.

As my assistant and I were checking the ballroom before the guests went in, we saw that there was a leak in the party room ceiling, and water was dripping right onto a chair. Fortunately, we were able to move the table slightly to avoid having the guests get wet.

The wedding was held at a beautiful old mansion, with the ceremony outdoors and the reception both inside and out. The problem was that the heat index was supposed to be at 104 degrees. The father of the bride was panicked, so we quickly arranged to have electric fans for the outdoor space near the ceremony, cold washcloths for guests, and chilled bottled water available for all. It was unbelievably hot, but happily, all went well.

When we got to the church, I called the florist because everything that had been ordered did not appear. One wrist corsage was missing, but there was no time for the florist to bring another, so I took several long-stemmed yellow calla lilies from an arrangement and tied them together for the bride's sister.

At one wedding, as the ceremony was ending, my assistant went outside to check on the transportation and came back in a panic. The trolley driver and I had discussed where to keep his vehicle during the ceremony, and I had suggested that he keep it down the block a bit, but he had moved his vehicle onto the sidewalk instead, and the left front tire had gone into a pothole and couldn't get out. The vehicle was now stuck, and we had no transportation back to the reception for the bridal party. We made the announcement and suggested that they all take taxis and give the receipts to us. We also called the trolley company directly, and a representative actually came out to the hotel to speak with the bride. Now that's good service.

For one wedding, the rehearsal was scheduled for seven o'clock at night in a historic church. I was there ahead of time, and as it got closer to seven, the huge bridal party (nine bridesmaids, twelve groomsmen) trickled in—but no bride. Thirty minutes later, still no bride. Finally, one of the bridesmaids got a call, and I was told that the hotel had misplaced the bride's gown in another guest room, and the bride was hysterical. I'm not quite sure why the bride didn't come straight to the rehearsal and let the hotel find the dress, but she didn't, and she arrived at the church about forty minutes late. And yes, the hotel did find the dress, and it was waiting for her in her room when she got back.

One wedding day turned out to be very windy. Several windows were open in the ballroom, and four flower arrangements were blown over. Fortunately, this was during the setup period, and the windows were closed, and the arrangements were set in place.

For one wedding, the bride had worked with the florist to design tall centerpieces that included high branches with votive candles hanging down. Inside each glass fixture was a candle and some moss. The effect was gorgeous, but early during the dinner service, the moss in one of them caught fire. The venue had to have us extinguish all of them immediately.

The wedding director at the ceremony told me to hit a particular button to signal the start of the music and alert the organist to start playing. Then she told me that I should hit the button twice to change to the music for the processional. She departed at that point, and the ceremony got under way. I cued the organist and processional just as instructed, and then I left to go downstairs to do other tasks. But she never told me that I had to cue the organist to *stop* playing after everyone was down the aisle. I assumed that he would just play "Canon in D" and end it in the usual way, but that's not what happened. The organist went on and on. My assistant finally figured out that she needed to hit another button, and she did it. There was a little laugh by all, I think, but thank goodness my assistant was able to figure it out.

After the recessional, the bride and groom hid on a staircase behind a door at the back of the church so the guests could go outside and wait for the presentation of the couple. Then there was to be a sword ceremony by the groom's Navy buddies. But the bride and groom closed the door where they were hiding, and it locked, so they couldn't get out! I ran to find the sacristan, and then I couldn't find the swordsmen. Through the door, I asked the groom where they might be, and he told me to look outside on the opposite side of the church ... and there they were.

We were on our way to a wedding and were already running late. The bridal party hustled out of the house, and the bride's dad closed the door. Then the bride panicked. She said she thought she was going to faint. I put smelling salts on the top of my car and told her she could use them if she wanted them (I never, ever hand out or dispense medication of any kind), and I also gave her a power bar for the car ride. Then she said that she didn't have her house keys and that the house had been closed up incorrectly, and the burglar alarm would be going off. There was not a thing we could do about it at that point, so we all piled into the sedan and limo and went to the church.

In the middle of one wedding, the caterer pulled me aside and told me that they had never been told that there was going to be a dessert wine served, so they had someone in the kitchen rinsing—not *washing*—glasses from earlier in the evening. I was slightly horrified, but I hadn't been told about the dessert wine, either, and there was nothing I could do.

When my assistant and I arrived at the reception venue, we noticed that the escort cards were not in alphabetical order. They were by table number instead, and we had never received (although we requested) a guest list. We frantically rushed to alphabetize them while the bridal party was having photos taken.

The groom's family wanted personalized ice sculptures, so the hotel had ordered four distinct ice carvings to be placed in various spaces at the cocktail reception. On one was the bride's name—*spelled wrong*. Fortunately, the bride had a great sense of humor about it and was okay.

Talk about attention to detail, or lack thereof: the mother of the bride gave a count to the hotel (181) and the florist (175)—and the place cards had 182 names. *Ugh.*

Somehow. one of the guests arrived in Philly without having booked a hotel room, and this was Labor Day weekend. My two assistants called every hotel they could think of, and every single place was booked. So we scrambled and called absolutely every little motel, bed-and-breakfast, and club we could think of, and we finally found a room.

I checked the tables at one wedding, and there were supposed to be three forks and two knives set at each place, per my notes. But the place settings only had one of each. Fortunately, I told the caterer, and it was adjusted in time.

At one summer wedding, it was so hot that the caterer told me that they might not be able to serve the chocolate mousse cake because it was melting. The cake was on display as guests sat down and then was moved to a refrigerator until it was time to be cut and served. I was glad the caterer was watching it carefully.

I happened to be standing near the escort card table, and a young man, wearing neither a jacket nor a tie, came up to me and said that he had no card. I went to the groom and asked if he knew this man, and he said yes, that he was a good friend. So the groom suggested four tables where I could possibly add a seat.

As it turned out, there were several other names that never made it on to the seating lists, including a well-known personality who was there in a wheelchair and had brought along his nurse. It took some rearranging, but at last we got everyone seated with a minimum of disruption.

Before the ceremony, the brother of the groom broke his boutonniere, so I left the stem of the rose pinned on and then pinned the head on separately. It worked, apparently, until cocktail time. Before the brother gave his speech, he saw me and told me that the rose had fallen apart. He went to the bathroom, and when he came back, I had already grabbed a rose from an enormous centerpiece on the escort card table, cut the stem off with my scissors, and produced a boutonniere pin, and as he walked by, I pinned it on. I never told him where I got it, but I was pretty pleased with myself for quick thinking.

When my assistant and I were on our way to the rehearsal, I received a call on my cell from the mother of the bride. She had forgotten to pick up the bride's wedding dress at a shop almost an hour away. I was already right around the corner from the venue, but I called the shop and asked how late they were open and how early they would open the next morning. They said they were closing shortly and they wouldn't be open until ten o'clock the next morning, and this was a noon wedding! When I reported back to the bride's mother, she said that her brother and sister-in-law would pick up the dress immediately, and we called the shop back to see if they could possibly stay open for a few extra minutes if necessary. They agreed, and the dress was retrieved.

The night before the wedding, the bride handed me the escort cards and envelopes and asked me to sort it all out. What a fiasco! It took me hours—I had to match and stuff the small cards with the correct table numbers, there weren't enough table number cards, the bride had added several more guests, and it was a general mess. For the new guests, she asked me to just write the names and numbers on the cards by hand, since we couldn't have them written in calligraphy in time. She said she didn't care if I used black ink, even though the cards were written in gold script. I thought about it and decided that this was *not* happening on my watch. I knew I needed a gold pen.

The next day, I started out by calling the hotel's concierge to ask where I could find a gold pen. He told me that Staples, which was somewhere nearby, opened at nine o'clock and would have one. He gave me a car and driver, and off I went. No gold calligraphy pen, but at least they did have a slim gold marker. A lesson learned: always find out the color of the calligraphy on the escort cards ahead of time, and have a pen ready.

One mother of the bride asked me to put two gardenias that were wired for the bride's hair in the refrigerator. I asked someone from the venue where the refrigerator was, and he brought me to it and opened the door. The only thing inside was a plate of shaped pats of butter, so I put the flowers in.

When I went to retrieve them after the ceremony so the bride could have them for the photos now that her veil was off, I took the flowers out, and they were frozen—and when they came up to room temperature, they browned immediately. Oh my. What to do? Fortunately, the florist was still there, so I asked her for replacement flowers. She had no more gardenias but offered (thank goodness!) to wire some orchids, which she did. When the bride asked for the flowers, I told her that there had been a little mishap with the gardenias and put the orchids in her hair, which actually looked even better. She was happy, and the wedding photos and celebration went on as planned.

The banquet captain came up to me after the bride and groom cut the (very expensive, very fancy) cake to tell me that the cake was all vanilla, not half vanilla and half chocolate as ordered. He was panicky and had no backup. He begged me to be the one to tell the mother of the bride. I did, and she was cool with it. I think it took the banquet captain some time to relax after that close call.

I saw the banquet manager as I came upstairs to the party area, and he said that he didn't have the correct jack for the iPod that was to provide music for the cocktail reception. I'm not sure why he didn't check it out beforehand, but he spent a very long time trying to figure it out. He did get the music up and running, but it meant that the band ate dinner late, and we had to rearrange the timeline.

Unfortunately, one wedding guest (a friend of the groom's parents) tripped on her gown at the reception and had to go to the hospital with a broken wrist. The next day, the groom's mother called the bride's mother to tell her that the guest, her friend of forty years, was planning to sue the venue *and* the bride's parents regarding the injury! Of course, the friendship ended immediately, and there was ultimately a lawsuit that was settled by the insurance companies involved.

Some of the Lucite candleholders on the dinner tables started to burn from the heat of the flames. They had four candles in them and actually started to smoke, so the wedding director and hotel staff hurriedly removed them. Catastrophe averted!

One wedding took place outside on a hot and muggy day, and the wedding cake started falling into itself on one side. The baker was called back before dinner to fix it, and she tried. She took the layers apart, put more straws in, and piped more icing at the joints of the layers. But even that didn't help much—it was so humid outside—and finally we all had to recognize that the cake just wasn't going to make it. The caterer ended up putting it in the refrigerator during the meal so that the bride and groom would have something to cut later.

When I arrived at the venue, it had a large LOVE ice sculpture in place—which would have been great, except that the bride and groom had ordered one with their initials. I asked the banquet manager about it, and he went to the freezer and pulled out the right one.

I was in the hallway outside of the bride's getting-ready room and saw the father of the bride storm down the hall. Then his teary, slightly hysterical wife came out. She said that all her jewelry was missing. As it turned out, the bride had it all. It was too bad that there had to be this upset and drama.

The grandmother of the bride was getting ready to walk down the aisle, and she was wearing a wrist corsage, except that somehow, in a short period of time and in a confined space, she had lost the flower. I always request an extra boutonniere for a wedding, so I took the wristband to my staging area, turned on my glue gun, and quickly attached a boutonniere to the band. She had a lovely corsage to walk down the aisle, after all, and no one else knew.

The bride and groom had ordered a stage for the *mandap*, a covered structure with pillars under which a Hindu or Jain wedding takes place, for the ceremony venue. I assumed they knew what they were ordering, but no. The stage that arrived had ugly gray carpeting, and it looked terrible with the vibrant pink draping on the mandap. What to do? The venue didn't have anything else, and it was too late to rent something, so I asked the concierge for four king-size ivory sheets and gave them to the amazing florist who pulled them tight and secured them on top of the mandap stage.

The videographer asked if I had any Febreze. I had no clue why he needed it, but I sent my intern across the street to Walgreens to buy some. When I saw him again, he told me that he had spilled coffee on himself on the way to the hotel and that he had reeked of coffee. So instead, he spent the wedding reeking of Febreze.

I am often asked if I can tell whether a marriage will last by looking at the couple. The answer is no, of course, as I can't begin to know all the details of an entire relationship, but there were a few times where I sensed trouble. At one, the bride and groom were seated at a sweetheart table for their wedding reception. When their entrées were served, the groom was nowhere to be found. He had walked out of the room and had not reappeared. The bride sat at the table for two all alone—no groom in sight. I watched as a bridesmaid came over to the bride, picked up her dinner plate, and brought the food and the bride to her table. The groom was gone for at least an hour. At another wedding, the groom didn't want to be in the photos. He resisted and was extremely difficult. Both couples are now divorced.

One father of the groom came up to me after the couple had been introduced at the reception and said that he was pissed (his words) because the first dance song was "Let's Call the Whole Thing Off." I spoke to the bandleader, and he just laughed. The bride and groom had specifically chosen that song—it was their private joke.

Once the guests had come into the ballroom, the catering manager came over to me and said that there were twelve people trying to be seated at a table for ten. The manager asked if I could check the guests' names. I went around and found out which couple was at the wrong table and then checked another list to find out where they were supposed to be. The woman literally grabbed the paper from my hand and said she wanted to see who else was at her table—because maybe she didn't want to sit there!

The venue gave the family *two* tastings instead of the customary one. Even so, on the day of the wedding, the mother of the bride wanted me *and* the catering manager to taste the food before it was served to make sure there wasn't too much salt.

One guest didn't RSVP, but it wasn't a problem, as the bride had directed that an extra table be set for six because she had "casually invited" some other guests to attend.

A staff person came to tell me that one of the guests didn't have an escort card. The name was not on my list, so I had to go to the groom—who was in the middle of a photo session—to check. He assured me that this friend was invited, but apparently, he had changed his name and was listed under his "new" name at table 16.

This was a first: wedding crashers! A local university was holding an event in the same hotel and on the same floor as the wedding, so there were some young men who tried to join the party in the ballroom. We stopped them, but still. As I was setting up the escort cards, one of these men put a drink that he had (mostly) finished down on the tablecloth. Um … I don't think so.

When I went back into the ballroom at the end of the night, I literally stumbled on a crumpled-up napkin on the floor. I bent down to pick it up, and inside was the glass that the groom had stepped on during the wedding ceremony. I was so glad that I had found it, as it was supposed to be a keepsake for the couple!

Acknowledgments

I am so appreciative of the brides, grooms, partners, parents, wedding parties, wedding professionals, and clergy and officiants, as well as the unsung heroes who make deliveries, pick up dirty linens, serve the food and drinks, build and dismantle decor, and perform their services behind the scenes and without cheers and thanks. You make my job exciting, challenging, rewarding, and, of course, possible. I love being part of a couple's and their families' special day, and I am privileged to work with you.

Thank you all.

And, most of all, to my family, my deepest gratitude and love. As a wise man used to say, "Every day is a good day. Some are just better than others." You make my every day the best.

About the Author

Lynda Barness launched I DO Wedding Consulting in 2004 as her "encore career" after a successful and award-winning career as a real estate developer and home builder. She completed the certificate program in Wedding Planning and Consulting at Temple University and has achieved the designation of Master Wedding Planner by the Association of Bridal Consultants. Lynda was recognized in 2010 as the International Society of Event Specialists (ISES) Best Wedding Planner in the Greater Philadelphia region and has had weddings published in *Philadelphia Wedding*, *Brides Philadelphia*, *Martha Stewart Weddings*, and more. She has planned weddings in Pennsylvania, New Jersey, Delaware, and also in London, England.